THREE BOOKS

ALSO BY GALWAY KINNELL

Poetry

What a Kingdom It Was   1960
Flower Herding on Mount Monadnock   1964
Body Rags   1968
First Poems 1946–1954   1971
The Book of Nightmares   1971
The Avenue Bearing the Initial of Christ
     into the New World: Poems 1946–64   1974
Mortal Acts, Mortal Words   1980
Selected Poems   1982
The Past   1985
When One Has Lived a Long Time Alone   1990

Prose

Black Light   1966
Walking Down the Stairs: Selections from Interviews   1978
How the Alligator Missed Breakfast (for children)   1982

Translations

Bitter Victory (novel by René Hardy)   1956
The Poems of François Villon   1965
On the Motion and Immobility of Douve
     (poems by Yves Bonnefoy)   1968
Lackawanna Elegy (poems by Yvan Goll)   1970
The Poems of François Villon (second version)   1977

Edition

The Essential Whitman   1987

GALWAY KINNELL

THREE BOOKS

BODY RAGS

MORTAL ACTS
MORTAL WORDS

THE PAST

Houghton Mifflin Company

BOSTON   NEW YORK

1993

Three Books: Copyright © 1993 by Galway Kinnell
Body Rags: Copyright © 1965, 1966, 1967 by Galway Kinnell
Mortal Acts, Mortal Words: Copyright © 1980 by Galway Kinnell
The Past: Copyright © 1985 by Galway Kinnell

For information about permission to reproduce selections from this book, write to
Permissions, Houghton Mifflin Company, 215 Park Avenue South, New York,
New York 10003.

Acknowledgments appear on p. 201.

Library of Congress Cataloging-in-Publication Data

Kinnell, Galway, date.
    [Poems. Selections]
    Three books / Galway Kinnell.
        p.   cm.
    Includes index.
    Contents: Body rags — Mortal acts, mortal words — The past.
    ISBN 0-395-68088-3 (pbk)   ISBN 0-395-68089-1 (cl)
    I. Title.
    PS3521.I582A6   1993
    811'.54 — dc20   93-5009
                            CIP

Printed in the United States of America

HAD 10 9 8 7 6 5 4 3 2 1

CONTENTS

MORTAL ACTS, MORTAL WORDS

I

II

III

THE PAST

I

II

III

A NOTE ON THE REVISIONS

Not very long ago, in an introduction I wrote to *The Essential Whitman*, I reproached Whitman for damaging his poems by continual revision, and I went so far as to articulate a Law of Elapsed Time:

> All writers know this law: revision succeeds in inverse ratio to the amount of time passed since the work was written. Revision is most likely to improve a poem when it directly follows composition, because it is, in fact, a slower, more reflective phase of the creative act. It is most likely to fail if many years have passed — such as the quarter century between the first publication and the last revision of *Leaves of Grass*. The only exception to the law is that ill-written and extraneous material may be excised with good effect at any time.

Some readers may notice that I have gone ahead and revised many poems in this book anyway, even though some were first published even longer ago than a quarter century; and they may wonder why I would announce this stern rule only to flout it at the first opportunity.

In explanation, I should say that not every revision in this book is really a revision. One was a correction of a twenty-five-year-old typographical error — over which I hesitated, out of admiration as if for a petty criminal who has eluded apprehension for a very long time, or because of some grandfather clause of the mind which momentarily stayed my hand.

Some of the revisions are in fact restitutions. In "Saint Francis and the Sow," for instance, I restored a word which I had taken out a dozen years ago when I put the poem into my *Selected Poems*. At that time I thought to myself, "Can a pig really have a broken heart?" and I changed "broken" to "unbreakable." Now I think I was right in the first place, and that my earlier scruple came from the harmful and surely false idea, carefully nurtured by our kind, that there is no resonance between our emotional life and that of the other animals.

The majority of the revisions are, I hope, simply deletions of "ill-written and extraneous material," and thus exempt, according to the Law, from the consequences of belated revision. These deletions are reasonably short except for one entire eleven-line section, which I removed from a poem called "The Poem" on the grounds that it seemed written more by habit than by conviction and, in any case, did not appear to move the poem forward.

Most of the material I took out could be described as familiar refrains, clotted conceits, fanciful elaborations, overemphases, exaggerations, willed sweetness, willed misery, wishfulness, grandiloquence, redundancies, irrelevancies, whimsies, pointlessly elaborate sound effects, contrived usages, efforts to enliven through heightened language what would have been lively if given straight, attempts to enliven what remains intractably dull, bravura cadenzas by the professor of creative writing.

I wished I could have simply deleted all material of this kind without replacing it, but some deletions left gaps. As I filled them, using plain language and straightforward syntax as much as possible, I realized that many of the instances of ill-written material mentioned above, which had seemed matters of style, were, at bottom, problems of truthfulness and accuracy. As I worked, I found I was trying less to correct flaws of phrasing than to discover what was going on and to articulate it through words' meanings, mouthfeel, and music. This was no longer mere deletion; this was rewriting, the kind of revision that is full of risk.

If rewritten material improves the poem only a little, it is likely to make the poem worse. When you substitute what seems like a splendid new passage for an old awkward one, in a poem that has been apparently finished for many years, it may seem that you have lifted it at last out of mediocrity; but when you look in on it the next day, you may find it lying in ruins. That is because there is a poetic equivalent to the organ transplant rejection syndrome. The new passage often won't cohere with the rest — in mood, in language, even in intent — and for better or worse the poem must make do with the original lines. In going over the poems in this book I tried to rewrite only when I felt sure the revision would stick.

Paul Valéry said that poets do not finish their poems, they abandon them. I don't know how this statement strikes other poets, but it rings true for me at least in regard to a number of long and, from my point of view, complicated poems, such as some of the longer poems in Part III of *The Past*. When that book was published I might have had an inkling that some poems were not completely right, but I felt I had taken them as far as it was in my power to do. When the idea of *Three Books* was proposed, I was happy to have another chance to see if I could do any better by them. I was not expecting, however, to be able to enter these poems as easily and fully as, at moments, I did.

Retiring athletes sometimes say something like, "With what I now know about the game, I could *really* play, if only I still had my legs." At least a few times, working on these poems, I fell into deep concentration and felt as if I were back there, then, in the full heat of composition — that I had, at those moments, the legs of a young man again — and knowing what I now know — having waked up, in certain ways, to the need to surmount the perspective ingrained in us and built into our use of language, which usually puts the self in the center and others dimly at the margins, for instance, and to the realization that the ability to say the beautiful is not completely separate from the ability to say the ugly — I believed I could now, by a change here or there, carry those poems a degree further toward completion.

It sometimes seems to me, that there must be few poets who revise more than I do, and that this impulse in me may be a kind of illness, perhaps the kind we have when we are unable to acknowledge any limits or, deeper down than we know, accept time and death. But if so, the illness can be unexpectedly pleasurable and may even do the poems some good. In going over "Last Holy Fragrance" I became totally absorbed in it — as if, years after I started it, I were still in the midst of writing it — and realized that I now knew why James Wright's eyes sometimes opened wide for a second when he was reading his poems aloud. I realized it when I came to this passage in which I tell how, as I read his work aloud,

> sometimes
> I hear *only* his voice, edged, pitying,
> surprising language with the mourning
> that goes on inside it, for what it names,
> making my eyes "pop" a little, perhaps
> showing the whites, as his used to,
> when the poems were at their saddest.

On reaching the last line I struck it out without thinking and wrote in:

when his own poems startled him.

I am grateful to the occasion of *Three Books* for letting me get this and perhaps a few other things right.

GALWAY KINNELL
New York City
1993

BODY RAGS

TO INÉS

PART I

ANOTHER NIGHT IN THE RUINS

1

In the evening
haze darkening on the hills,
purple
of the eternal, a last bird
crosses over, *'flop flop'*,
adoring
only the instant.

2

Nine years ago,
in a plane that rumbled all night
above the Atlantic,
I could see, lit up
by lightning bolts jumping out of it,
a thunderhead formed like the face
of my brother, looking nostalgically down
on blue,
lightning-flashed moments of the Atlantic.

3

He used to tell me,
"What good is the day?
On some hill of despair
the bonfire
you kindle can light the great sky —
though it's true, of course, to make it burn
you have to throw yourself in . . ."

4

Wind tears itself hollow
in the eaves of my ruins, ghost-flute
of snowdrifts
that build out there in the dark:
upside-down
ravines into which night sweeps
our torn wings, our ink-spattered feathers.

5

I listen.
I hear nothing. Only
the cow, the cow
of nothingness, mooing
down the bones.

6

Is that a
rooster? He
thrashes in the snow
for a grain. Finds
it. Rips
it into
flames. Flaps. Crows.
Flames
bursting out of his brow.

7

How many nights must it take
one such as me to learn
that we aren't, after all, made
from that bird which flies out of its ashes,
that for a man
as he goes up in flames, his one work
is
to open himself, to *be*
the flames?

LOST LOVES

1

On ashes of old volcanoes
I lie dreaming,
baking
the deathward flesh in the sun,

and dream I can hear
a door, far away,
banging softly in the wind:

Mole Street. Quai-aux-Fleurs. Françoise.
Greta. "After Lunch" by Po Chu-I.
"The Sunflower" by Blake.

2

And yet I can rejoice
that everything changes, that
we go from life
into life,

and enter ourselves
quaking
like the tadpole, his time come, tumbling toward the slime.

GETTING THE MAIL

I walk back
toward the frog pond, carrying
the one letter, a few wavy lines
crossing the stamp: tongue-streaks
from the glue
and spittle beneath: my sign.

The frogs'
eyes bulge toward the visible, suddenly
an alderfly glitters past, declining
to die: her third giant step
into the world.

And touching
the name stretched over the envelope
like a blindfold, I wonder,
what did *getting warm* used to mean? And tear

open the letter
to the far-off, serene
groans of a cow
a farmer is milking in the August dusk
and the Kyrie of a chainsaw drifting down off Wheelock Mountain.

VAPOR TRAIL REFLECTED
IN THE FROG POND

1

The old watch: their
thick eyes
puff and foreclose by the moon. The young, heads
trailed by the beginnings of necks,
shiver,
in the guarantee they shall be bodies.

In the frog pond
the vapor trail of a SAC bomber creeps,

I hear its drone, drifting, high up
in immaculate ozone.

2

And I hear,
coming over the hills, America singing,
her varied carols I hear:
crack of deputies' rifles practicing their aim on stray dogs at night,
sput of cattleprod,
TV groaning at the smells of the human body,
curses of the soldier as he poisons, burns, grinds, and stabs
the rice of the world,
with open mouth, crying strong, hysterical curses.

3

And by rice paddies in Asia
bones
wearing a few shadows
walk down a dirt road, smashed

bloodsuckers on their heel, knowing
the flesh a man throws down in the sunshine
dogs shall eat
and the flesh that is upthrown in the air
shall be seized by birds,
shoulder blades smooth, unmarked by old feather-holes,
hands rivered
by blue, erratic wanderings of the blood,
eyes crinkled up
as they gaze up at the drifting sun that gives us our lives,
seed dazzled over the blaze of the earth.

THE FOSSILS

1

In the cliff over the frog pond
I clawed in the flagmarl and stones,
crushed up
lumps half grease half dust:
atrypas came out,
lophophyllidiums casting shadows,
corals bandaged in wrinkles,
wing-shaped allorismas,
sea-lily disks . . .
which did not molder into dust
but held.

Night rose up
in black smoke, making me
blind. My fingertips rubbed
smooth on my brain, I knelt in the dark, cracking
the emptiness,
poking spirifers into flying black dust,
letting sylvan remains slither through my fingers,
whiffing the glacial roses,
feeling the pure absence of the ephemera . . .

And shall
I have touched
the ornithosuchus, whose wings
try, not to evade earth, but to press closer to it?

2

While Bill Gratwick flapped, pranced
and called the dances,

light-headed
as a lizard on hind legs I sashayed
with Sylvia, of the woods, as woodwinds
flared and crackled in the leaves,
Sylph-ia, too, of that breeze
for whom even the salamander rekindles wings;
and I danced the eighteenth-century shoulder-rub
with Lucy,
my shoulder blades starting to glitter
on hers as we turned, sailbacks
in laired and changing dance,
our faces smudged with light from the fingertips of the ages.

3
Outside
in dark fields
I pressed the coiled
ribs of a fingerprint to a stone,
first light in the flesh.

Over the least fossil
day breaks in gold, frankincense, and myrrh.

THE BURN

Twelve years ago I came here
to wander across burnt land,
I had only begun to know
the kind of pain others endure,
I was too full of sorrows.
Now, on the dirt road
that winds beside the Kilchis River
to the sea, saplings
on all the hills, I go deep
into the first forest of Douglas firs
shimmering out of prehistory,
a strange shine up where the tops
shut out the sky, whose roots
feed in the waters of the rainbow trout.
And here, at my feet, in the grain
of a burnt log opened by a riverfall,
the clear
swirls of the creation. At the
San Francisco airport, Charlotte,
where yesterday my arms
died around you like old snakeskins, the puffed
needletracks on your arms
marked how the veins wander.
I see you walking like a somnambulist
through a poppy field, blind
as myself on this dirt road, tiny
flowers brightening about you,
the skills of fire, of fanning
the blossoms until they die,

perfected; only the power to nurture
and make whole, only love,
impossible. The mouth of the river.
On these beaches
the sea throws itself down, in flames.

ONE WHO USED TO BEAT HIS WAY

Down the street of warehouses,
each with
its redlighted shaftway,
its Corinthian columns,
its bum crapped out on the stoop,
he staggers, among
wraiths that steam up out of manhole covers
and crimesheets skidding from the past.

He gets a backed-up
mouthful of vomit-cut liquor, mumbles, "Thanks God,"
and regulps it. And
behind him the continent glimmers, the wild land
crossed by the *Flying Crow*
that changed her crew at Shreveport,
the *Redball* and the *Dixie Flyer*, that went on through,
the *Big 80*
that quilled her whistles to make blues on the Delta.
"Everybody's eating everybody, and nobody
gives a shit where they bite,"
the old timer growls, poking the jungle fire . . .
"Bible-ranters, bulls, hicks, systems, scissor-bills . . ."

And he who used
to beat his way hauls himself down
into his niche, where he has left his small possessions,
a killed bottle,
a streamed of piss groping down the dry stone.

THE FLY

1

The fly
I've just brushed
from my face keeps buzzing
about me, flesh-
eater
starved for the soul.

One day I may learn to suffer
his mizzling, sporadic stroll over eyelid and cheek,
even seize on his burnt
singing with joy.

2

The bee is beautiful.
She is the fleur-de-lys in the flesh.
She has a tuft of the sun on her back.
She brings sexual love to the narcissus flower.
She sings of fulfillment
and stings and dies.
And everything she ever touches
is opening! opening!

And yet we say our last goodbye
to the fly last,
the flesh-fly last,
the absolute last,
the naked dirty reality of him last.

ANGO

opens in three: yellow-gold
  dawn
the mudwalls of Hafez' garden,
a seagull mewing for the light,

stere,
nacking of turpentine,
ringy, like flesh.

Under
he mango limbs
verfilled with flesh,
few old women squat by the whitening sea,
lapping, chorusing of love.

THE FALLS

The elemental murmur
as they plunge, *croal, croal,*
and *haish, haish,* over
the ledges,
through stepless wheels
and bare axles, down between
sawmills that have
buckled and slid sideways to their knees . . .

When I fall I would fall to my sounding . . .
the lowly,
unchanged, stillic, rainbowed sounding
of the Barton River Falls.

IN THE ANSE GALET VALLEY

1

Clouds
rise by twos out of the jungle, cross
under the moon, and sink
into
the peak called Font-des-Serpents.

I remember the child's game:
angel's wings,
laid-open scallop shell,
gowpen overspilling milled grain,
two moles feeling their way through the light,
myself and . . .

2

A straw torch
flickers
far off among the trees,
of a nightfisherman
wading upstream clubbing the fishes.

The fer-de-lances
writhe in black winding-skins,
the grail-bearers go down, dissolving.
What question could I have asked, the wafer-
moon
gnawed already at its death-edge?

LA BAGARÈDE

1

I take the dogs into
town and buy chèvre and a bâtard.
Back at La Bagarède I eat
this little meal in the dusk
and sit a long time, until

the Swan grows visible, trailing
her indicated wings down the horizon,
and Orion
begins to stalk the last nights of the summer.

2

The black
water I gulp from the spring
hits my brain at the root. And
I can hear
the giant, dark blooms of sunflowers
crackling open. And in the sky
the seventh
of the Sisters, she who hid herself
for shame
at having loved one who dies, is shining.

NIGHT IN THE FOREST

1

A woman
sleeps next to me on the earth. A strand
of hair flows
from her cocoon sleeping bag, touching
the ground hesitantly, as if thinking
to take root.

2

I can hear
a mountain brook
and somewhere blood winding
down its ancient labyrinths. And
a few feet away
charred stick-ends surround
a bit of ashes, where burnt-out, vanished flames
absently
waver, absently leap.

GOING HOME BY LAST LIGHT

1

Redheaded by last light,
with high-stepped, illusionist amble
I walk toward the white room
where she is waiting,
past
pimentos,
red cabbages,
tomatoes flickering in their bins,
past melons, past mushrooms and onions.

2

Those swarms
of Mayflies that used to rise
at the Vermont threshold, "imagos"
thrown up for a day,
their mouths shriveling closed,
their wings,
their sexual parts, newborn and perfect . . .

3

For several minutes
two mosquitoes have been making love
on top of this page,
changing positions, swooning, even they,
their thighs
fragile as a baby's hairs, knowing
the ecstasy.

4
A day!
The wings of the earth
lift and fall
to the groans, the cold, savage thumpings of a heart.

HOW MANY NIGHTS

How many nights
have I lain in terror,
O Creator Spirit, Maker of night and day,

only to walk out
the next morning over the frozen world
hearing under the creaking of snow
faint, peaceful breaths . . .
snake,
bear, earthworm, ant . . .

and above me
a wild crow crying *'yaw yaw yaw'*
from a branch nothing cried from ever in my life.

LAST SONGS

1

What do they sing, the last birds
coasting down the twilight,
banking
across woods filled with darkness, their
frayed wings
curved on the world like a lover's arms
which form, night after night, in sleep,
an irremediable absence?

2

Silence. Ashes
in the grate. Whatever it is
that keeps us from heaven,
sloth, wrath, greed, fear, could we only
reinvent it on earth
as song.

IN THE FARMHOUSE

1

Eaves moan,
clapboards flap,

behind me the potbellied
stove,
Ironside #120, rusty, cracked,
rips thick chunks of birchwood
into fire.

2

Soon it will be spring,
again the vanishing of the snows,

and tonight
I sit up late, mouthing
the sounds that would be words
in this flimsy jew's-harp of a farmhouse
in the wind
rattling on the twelve lights of blackness.

THE CORRESPONDENCE SCHOOL INSTRUCTOR SAYS GOODBYE TO HIS POETRY STUDENTS

Goodbye, lady in Bangor, who sent me
snapshots of yourself, after definitely hinting
you were beautiful; goodbye,
Miami Beach urologist, who enclosed plain
brown envelopes for the return of your *very*
"Clinical Sonnets"; goodbye, manufacturer
of brassieres on the Coast, whose eclogues
give the fullest treatment in literature yet
to the sagging breast motif; goodbye, you in San Quentin,
who wrote, "Being German my hero is Hitler,"
instead of "Sincerely yours," at the end of long,
neat-scripted letters demolishing
the pre-Raphaelites:

I swear to you, it was just my way
of cheering myself up, as I licked
the stamped, self-addressed envelopes,
the game I had
of trying to guess which one of you, this time,
had poisoned the glue. I did care.
I did read each poem entire.
I did say what I thought was the truth
in the mildest words I knew. And now,
in this poem, or chopped prose, not any better,
I realize, than those troubled lines

I kept sending back to you,
I have to say I am relieved it is over:
at the end I could feel only pity
for that urge toward more life
your poems kept smothering in words.

THE POEM

1

On this hill crossed
by the last birds, a sprinkling
of soil covers up the rocks
with green, as
the face
drifts on a skull scratched with glaciers.

The poem too
is a palimpsest, streaked
with erasures, smelling
of departure and burnt stone.

2

The full moon
slides from the clouds, the trees'
graves all lie out at their feet:

the leaf
shaped tongue
of the new born and the dying
quivers, and no one interprets it.

3

Where is "The Apocalypse of Lamech"?
Where is the "Iliupersis"?
Where is the "Khavadhaynamagh"?
Where is the "Rommant du Pet au Deable"?

Where is "The Book of the Lion"?
Where is the servantose of the sixty girls of Florence?
Where are the small poems Li Po folded into boats and pushed out on
    the river?
Where are the snows that fell in these graves?

4

On a branch
in the morning light, at the tip
of an icicle,the letter C
comes into being — trembles,
to drop, or to cling?

Suddenly a roman
carapace glitters all over it. Look:

5

Here is a fern-leaf binding *utter* to the image of *illume,*
here is a lightning-split fir the lines down its good side becoming whit-
    manesque and free,
here is *unfulfilled* reflected as *mellifica* along the feather of a crow,
here is a hound chasing his bitch in trochaic dimeter brachycatalectic,
here are the pits where the tongue-bone is hurled at its desolate cry,
here are my own clothes composing *emptiness* in khaskura,
here is a fly convulsing down the poisoned labyrinth of this hand-
    writing,
here is an armful of last-year's-snows.

6

The moment
in the late night, when baby birds
closed in dark wings almost stir, and objects
on the page grow suddenly
heavy, hugged
by a rush of strange gravity:

the surgery of the funeral
and of the funeral oration, the absence

in the speech I will have left in the world
of

7
Where are "The Onions"
that I saw swollen with tears on a grocery shelf
in 1948?

brong ding plang ching of a spike
driven crazy on a locust
post.

PART II

THE LAST RIVER

1

When I cross
on the high, back-reared ferry boat
all burnished brass and laboring pistons
and look at the little tugs and sticklighters
and the great ships from foreign lands
and wave to a deckhand gawking at the new world
of sugar cane and shanties and junked cars
and see a girl by the ferry rail,
the curve the breeze makes down her thigh,
and the green waves lighting up . . .
the cell-block
door crawls open and they fling us a pimp.

2

The lights dim,
the dirty jokes die out.

Rumble of trailertrucks
on Louisiana 1 . . . I think
of the rides
back from the courthouse in Amite,
down the canyon between
faces smiling from the billboards,
the car filled
with black men who tried to register to vote . . .
Tickfaw . . . Independence . . . Albany . . .

Moan of
a riverboat creeping
upstream . . . yap and screech
of police dogs
attacking the police in their dreams.

3

Under the blue flasher
and the siren's wail, the prisoner
gazes out at anything,
anything at all of the world . . .
surreal spittoon . . .
glow of EAT . . .
fresh-hit carcass . . . cat . . . coon . . .
polecat . . .

and lightning flashes,
path strung out a moment across the storm,
bolt even made of hellfire
between any strange life and any strange life,
blazed
for those who shudder in their beds
hearing a siren's wail
fading down a dead-ridden highway at night . . .
thump . . . armadillo . . . thump . . . dog . . .

4

Somebody wakes,
he's got himself a "nightcrawler" — one of those
jokes that come to you in your sleep —
about girls who have "cross-bones"
and can't, consequently,
be entered . . . An argument flares up
on whether there is, or is not,
a way to circumvent the cross-bone . . .
"Sheee-it! Sheee-it!" the copbeater cries,
and the carthief says, "Jeee-ziz! Jeee-ziz!"
"All right boys," the pimp puts in from time to time.
"What say? Let's get a little fucking sleep."

5

I turn on the iron bunk . . .
One day in Ponchatoula
when the IC from Chicago crept
into the weeds of the Deep South, and stopped,
I thought I saw three
of my kinsmen from the North
in the drinking car, boozing their way
down to New Orleans,
putting themselves across,
selling themselves,
dishing up soft soap,
plump, manicured, shit-eating, opulent, razor-sharp . . .

Then the train
lurched and pushed on, carrying them off,
Yankee . . . equalitarian . . .
grease in the palm of their golden aspirations.

6

When I think America consists
only of billboards that smile,
I think of my friends
out there,
from Plaquemine or Point Coupee,
who go from shanty to shanty
in the dust,
fighting to keep empty
the space in their breast, to trudge
through the dust for nothing,
nothing at all,

the dust
suddenly changed
into pollen of sunflowers, giving light at their feet.

7

The carthief's face,
oddly childish as he sleeps,

reminds me now of Jesus — a Jesus
I saw on a Negro funeral parlor calendar,
blue-eyed, rosy-cheeked, milky and soft . . .

I remember his beautiful speech of the old days . . .
those prayers, funeral orations, anthems,
war songs, and — actual poems! some of them
as beautiful as,
for example, "Wall Kill," "Terre Haute,"
"Stillwater," "Alcatraz" . . . under its name
each more escapeproof,
more supersecure,
more insane than the last,
liberty, said Shelley, being
"brightest in dungeons."

The carthief moans in his sleep, his face
now like a cat's.

8
Through the crisscross
of bars at the tiny window
I could see the swallows
that were darting in the last light,
late-flying creatures that surpass us in plain view . . .
bits of blurred flesh . . .
wavy lines . . .

Nothing's there now but a few stars
brightening
under the ice-winds of the emptiness . . .

Isn't it strange
that all love, all granting of respect,
has no face for its passing expressions but death's?

9

I hear now
the saddest of songs, the humming
the dew makes
as it dries from the garlic leaf.

A new night
and the dew will come back again,
for so many men and women
the chance to know justice
does not ever come.

10

I remember
the ancient ex-convict
who teaches voter-registration
in his shanty under the levee, standing
in the sun on the dirt road . . .
a crepe myrtle tree,
a passion flower,
a butterfly . . .

In the green, blistered sewer,
among beer cans, weeds, plastic flowers,
a few lumps of excrement, winged
with green flies.

The dust on the road
swirls up into little wing-shapes, that blow off,
the road made of dust goes down . . .

He smiles,
the air brightens as though ashes
of lightning bolts had been scattered through it.

What is it that makes the human face,
bit of secret,
lighted flesh, open up the earth?

11

A girl and I are lying
on the grass of the levee. Two
birds whirr overhead. We lie close,
as if having waked
in bodies of glory.

And putting on again
its skin of light, the river
bends into view. We watch it, rising
between the levees, flooding for the sky,
and hear it,
a hundred feet down, pressing its long weight
deeper into the world.

The birds have gone,
we wander slowly homeward, lost
in the history of every step . . .

12

I am a child
and I am lying face-down
by the Ten Mile River, one half mud
and one half piss, that runs
between the Seekonk Woods
and the red mills of Pawtucket
with their thousand windows and one smokestack,
breathing the burnt odor
of old rocks,
watching a bug breaking itself up,
holding
to my eye a bleached catfish
skull I turned up in the grass,
inside it, in the pit of light, a cross,

hearing the hornpout sounding
their horns mournfully deep inside the river.

13

Across
the dreamlit waters pushes
the flag-topped Plaquemine ferry,
and midway between shore and shore
it sounds its horn, and catfishes
of the Mississippi caterwaul and nose over,
heavy-skulled,
into the flinty, night-smelling depths.

14

All my life, of rivers
I hear
the longing cries, rut-roar
of shifted wind
on the gongs of beaten water . . .

the Ten Mile of Hornpout,
the Drac hissing in its bed of sand,
the Ruknabad crossed by ghosts of nightingales,
the Passumpsic bursting down its length in spring,
the East River of Fishes, the more haunting for not having had a past
    either,
and this Mississippi coursing down now through the silt of all its days,
and the Tangipahoa, snake-cracked, lifting with a little rush from the
    hills and going out in thick, undernourished greenery.

15

Was there some last
fling at grace in those eddies, some swirl
back toward sweet scraping, out there
where an Illinois cornstalk
drifts, turning the hours,
and the grinned skull of a boy?

The burning fodder dowses down,
seeking the snagged

bodies of the water-buried,
bits
of sainfoin sopped in fire, snuffed from below

down the flesh-dark Tallahatchie,
the bone-colored Pearl.

16

I wrench
a tassel of moss from a limb
to be my lightning-besom and sweep
the mists from the way.

Ahead of me a boy is singing,

　　didn't I ramble
　　I rambled
　　I rambled all around
　　in and out the town
　　I rambled
　　I rambled till the butcher cut me down . . .

He comes out of the mist,
he tells me his name is Henry David,
he takes my hand and leads me over the plain of crushed asphodels.

17

Who's this
at water's edge,
oar in hand, kneeling beside
his pirogue of blue stern . . .
no nose left,
no hair,
no teeth,
little points of flame for eyes,
limbs tied on with knots and rags?

"Let's go," I say, a big
salty wafer of spit in my mouth.

We step in
to the threshold groan, the pressurized
bayou water squirts in
at the seams, we oar out
on water brown-green
in the patches free of scum, nothing on all sides
but the old, quiet, curious diet of green,
alligatorwood,
swamp gum, tupelo, liquid amber,
live oak chrisomed in air-eating moss,
cypress risen among her failed roots . . .

18

Down here the air's
so thick with American radio-waves,
with our bare ears we can pick up
the groggy, backcountry announcers
drawling their pitch and hardsell
at old men forgotten under armies of roaches,
at babies with houseflies on lips and eyelashes,
at young men without future puking up present and past,
at recidivists sentenced deep into the hereafter,
at wineheads with only their self loathing for arms,
at hillbilly boys encountering the anti-sweat ads,
at . . .
          "Listen!" says Henry David.
"Sheee-it! Sheee-it!" a cupreous-
throated copbeater is chattering far off in the trees.

19

On the shore four souls
cry out in pain, one is lashed
by red suspenders to an
ever-revolving wheel, one with
red patches on the seat of his pants

shrieks while paunchy vultures
stab at his bourbon-squirting liver,
one shade pushes uphill
a belly puffed up with blood-money
that crashes back and crushes him, another
stands up to his neck
in the vomit he caused the living to puke . . .

"Southern politicians," Henry David says,
"Yonder, in Junkie's Hollow,
you'll find Northern ones . . ." I see one,
formerly mayor of a great city, as he draws
a needle from his arm,
blood, bits
of testicle dribble from the puncture.

20

A man comes lurching
toward me with big mirrors for eyes,
"Sammich!" he cries and doubles up in laughter.
I remember him at once, from ten years ago,
in Chicago, on a Sunday
in a park on the death-scented South Side,
in the days before my own life had even begun,
when full of strut and happiness
this person came up and cried, "Sammich!"
and now he says, "A fight,
I was makin' the scene and the fuzz
did blast my fuckin' ass off." He laughs.
He is also crying. He shrinks back. "Hey,"
he calls, "thanks for that sammich that day . . .
fat white bastard . . . "

21

We come to a crowd, hornets
in their hair, worms in their feet.
"They weren't for anything or against anything,"
Henry David says, "they looked out
for themselves."

Three men trot beside us,
peddling bits of their flesh,
dishing up soft screams,
plump, manicured, shit-eating, opulent . . .

Underfoot a man
with stars on his shoulders
grapples in the slime with his Secretary of Profit.
I kick him off him and he gets up.
"I stood above all partisan squabbles,"
he howls,
flashes the grin
that so loved itself it sold itself to the whole world,
and plunges back into the slime, throttling his Secretary of Sanctimony.

22

We come to robed
figures bunched on their knees,
meek eyes rolled up. By twitches
in their throats we gather they're alive.
"Rafel mai ameck zabi almi," they intone together.

Down on all fours, like a cat
at his saucer of fresh cream, their leader,
blue-eyed, rosy-cheeked, milky and soft, laps
with big tongue at a mirror.

23

Off to one side there's a man
signing restrictive covenants with his fingernails
on a blackboard. "That one,"
says my guide, "was
well-meaning; he believed
in equality and supported the good causes;
he got a shock, when he found out
this place is run by logicians . . ."
Hearing us talk, the man half turns . . .
"Come on," I say, sweating, for I know him.

47

24

We pass
victims of the taste for blood
who were hanged by the mob
just as the law was about to hang them,
we pass victims of justice
who were hanged by the mob for having got
stays of execution, executive pardons, or fair trials,
we pass victims of sexual dread
who cover, as we approach, the scabs at their crotches.

Here and there we see
"unknown persons"
killed for "unknown reasons"
at the hands of "persons unknown" . . .

25

We come to a river
where many thousands kneel, sucking up
its cloudy water
in a kind of frenzy . . .

"What river is it?" I ask.
"The Mystic River," Henry David says,
"the Healing Stream free to all
that flows from Calvary's Mountain . . . the liquor
that makes you forget . . ."

"And what's over there,
on the far shore?" "That?"
he says. "That's Camp Ground . . ."

I turn to see the police whipping
a child who refuses to be born,
she shrieks
and scrambles for the riverbank
and stands
singing in a floating, gospel wail,
"Oh Death, he is a little man . . ."

"What's it like in Camp Ground?" I ask.

But in the mist I only hear,

> I rambled
> in and out the town
> didn't I ramble
> I rambled . . .

26

My brain rids itself of light,
at last it goes out completely,
slowly
slowly
a tiny cell far within it
lights up:

a man of noble face
sits on the iron bunk, wiping
a pile of knifeblades clean
in the rags of his body.
My old hero. Should I be surprised?

"Hard to wash off . . .
buffalo blood . . . Indian blood . . ." he mutters,
at each swipe singing, "*mein herz! mein herz!*"

"Why you," I ask him,
"you who, in your life, loathed our crimes?"

"Seeking love . . . love
without human blood in it,
that leaps above
men and women, flesh and erections,
which I thought I had found
in a Massachusetts gravel bank one spring . . .
seeking love . . .
failing to know I only loved"

— here he began to sing — "my purity,
mein herz! mein fucking *herz!"*

"Hey," somebody
from another cellblock shouts, "What say?
Sleep . . . sleep . . ."

The light goes out. In the darkness
a letter for the blind
arrives in my stunned hands.

Did I come all this way only for this, only
to feel out the world-braille of my complicity,
only to choke down this last poison wafer?

For Galway alone.
I send you my mortality.
Which leans out from itself, to spit on itself.
Which you would not touch.
All you have known.

27

On one bank
of the last river stands
a black man, on the other
a white man, on the water between
a man of no color,
body of beryl,
face of lightning,
eyes lamps of wildfire,
arms and feet of polished brass.

There will come an agony upon you
beyond any
this nation has known;
and at that time thy people,
given intelligence, given imagination, given love, given . . .

Here his voice falters, he drops
to his knees, he is
falling to pieces,
no nose left,
no hair,
no teeth,
limbs dangling from prayer-knots and rags,

waiting by the grief-tree
of the last river.

PART III

TESTAMENT OF THE THIEF

1

Under the forked
thief-shadow lunging by the breeze,
a coolie sits, resting,
having lugged
a sack of earth to this spot,
shirt open,
legs spread,
head lolled to one side,
sweat-trickles,
plants,
tiny animals,
stylized all over him.

2

And on good terms
with the claustrophobic pewk-worm,
the louse,
the nerve-wracked flea,

a beggar has sprawled
all day on the ground
whether from laziness or love, while waters

rustle in their blue grooves, and birds
ask,
     '*koja? koja?*'

3

"This fellow is a colonel,
the degenerate next to him is a cop,

the scarecrow in the coma is a highschool principal,
the one dyed yellow
is chief of the narcotics squad,
that meatsack smokes to bring his weight down,
the squat one
puffing tragically is a poet
broken by longing to be Minister of Finance.

"Me? I just fix
their pipes, and hang on, stabbing
my poor portion of the world
with skinny assbones, waiting for my favorite to come,
a mean little boy
who is my most glorious punishment yet.

"Oh once
I regretted my life,
the only regret I have left, the only
poignant one, is the way these days
they soak you for opium.

"Listen,
I may be washed up,
but when you think of me, mull over
this proverb, will you? *If
the cat had wings
he would gobble up every bird in the sky.*"

4
The wild rose dies,
the hollyhock dies,
the poppy does not come back,
the moth preens herself all season long
for her carnal moment.

And yet a rose
has tossed the corpse its perfume.
That
that bloated snout could catch it proves

the body, too,
has had its springs in paradise.

5
A breeze off the bazaar,
lotus,
wild olive,
gum tragacanth,
indigo, musk,
burnt seed of wild rue,
gillyflower . . .

Under the breeze, in the dusk,
the poor cluster at tiny
pushcarts of fire, eating
boiled beets,
gut,
tongue,
testicle,
cheeks, forehead, little feet.

Down this street
the thief used to ramble, picking his way
in his pajamas,
on just
this spot, after a meal, he would sleep,
the earth drawing
all his bones down close upon it.

Stop a moment, on his bones' dents,
stand without moving, listen
to the ordinary people
as they pass. They do not sing
of what is gone or to come, they sing of
the old testaments of their lives,
the little meals,
the airs,
the streets of our time.

6

"*Item*, to the opium master
dying in paradise: this nose,
in working disorder,
crazed
for the poison fumes of the real.

"*Item*, to the beggar
dumped on blue stone, gasping
as, one after one, girl friends
of his youth hallucinate his nap:
these bones, their
iron faithfulness to loss.

"*Item*, to the coolie
who trudges over the earth bearing
earth on his backbones,
whose skeleton
shall howl for its dust like any other
on the bitter slopes of the creation:
this
ultimate ruckus on the groan-meat."

7

Item, to the pewk-worm
who lives all his life in our flesh,
nuzzling along
through fat and lean, skinny and soft,
gnawing himself a peephole when lost, in buttock or cheek,
whom you can drag forth
only by winding him up on a matchstick
a quarter turn a day for the rest of your days:
this map of my innards.

THE PORCUPINE

1

Fatted
on herbs, swollen on crabapples,
puffed up on bast and phloem, ballooned
on willow flowers, poplar catkins, first
leafs of aspen and larch,
the porcupine
drags and bounces his last meal through ice,
mud, roses and goldenrod, into the stubbly high fields.

2

In character
he resembles us in seven ways:
he puts his mark on outhouses,
he alchemizes by moonlight,
he shits on the run,
he uses his tail for climbing,
he chuckles softly to himself when scared,
he's overcrowded if there's more than one of him per five acres,
his eyes have their own inner redness.

3

Digger of
goings across floors, of hesitations
at thresholds, of
handprints of dread
at doorpost or window jamb, he would
gouge the world
empty of us, hack and crater
it

until it is nothing, if that
could rid it of all our sweat and pathos.

Adorer of ax
handles aflow with grain, of arms
of Morris chairs, of hand
crafted objects
steeped in the juice of fingertips,
of surfaces wetted down
with fist grease and elbow oil,
of clothespins that have
grabbed our body rags by underarm and crotch . . .

Unimpressed — bored —
by the whirl of the stars, by *these*
he's astonished, ultra-
Rilkean angel!

for whom the true
portion of the sweetness of earth
is one of those bottom-heavy, glittering, saccadic
bits
of salt water that splash down
the haunted ravines of a human face.

4
A farmer shot a porcupine three times
as it dozed on a tree limb. On
the way down it tore open its belly
on a broken
branch, hooked its gut,
and went on falling. On the ground
it sprang to its feet, and
paying out gut heaved
and spartled through a hundred feet of goldenrod
before
the abrupt emptiness.

5

The Avesta
puts porcupine killers
into hell for nine generations, sentencing them
to gnaw out
each other's hearts for the
salts of desire.

I roll
this way and that in the great bed, under
the quilt
that mimics this country of broken farms and woods,
the fatty sheath of the man
melting off,
the self-stabbing coil
of bristles reversing, blossoming outward —
a red-eyed, hard-toothed, arrow-stuck urchin
tossing up mattress feathers,
pricking the
woman beside me until she cries.

6

In my time I have
crouched, quills erected,
Saint
Sebastian of the
scared heart, and been
beat dead with a locust club
on the bare snout.
And fallen from high places
I have fled, have
jogged
over fields of goldenrod,
terrified, seeking home,
and among flowers
I have come to myself empty, the rope
strung out behind me
in the fall sun
suddenly glorified with all my blood.

7

And tonight I think I prowl broken
skulled or vacant as a
sucked egg in the wintry meadow, softly chuckling, blank
template of myself, dragging
a starved belly through the lichflowered acres,
where
burdock looses the arks of its seed
and thistle holds up its lost blooms
and rosebushes in the wind scrape their dead limbs
for the forced-fire
of roses.

THE BEAR

1

In late winter
I sometimes glimpse bits of steam
coming up from
some fault in the old snow
and bend close and see it is lung-colored
and put down my nose
and know
the chilly, enduring odor of bear.

2

I take a wolf's rib and whittle
it sharp at both ends
and coil it up
and freeze it in blubber and place it out
on the fairway of the bears.

And when it has vanished
I move out on the bear tracks,
roaming in circles
until I come to the first, tentative, dark
splash on the earth.

And I set out
running, following the splashes
of blood wandering over the world.
At the cut, gashed resting places
I stop and rest,
at the crawl-marks
where he lay out on his belly

to overpass some stretch of bauchy ice
I lie out
dragging myself forward with bear-knives in my fists.

3
On the third day I begin to starve,
at nightfall I bend down as I knew I would
at a turd sopped in blood,
and hesitate, and pick it up,
and thrust it in my mouth, and gnash it down,
and rise
and go on running.

4
On the seventh day,
living by now on bear blood alone,
I can see his upturned carcass far out ahead, a scraggled,
steamy hulk,
the heavy fur riffling in the wind.

I come up to him
and stare at the narrow-spaced, petty eyes,
the dismayed
face laid back on the shoulder, the nostrils
flared, catching
perhaps the first taint of me as he
died.

I hack
a ravine in his thigh, and eat and drink,
and tear him down his whole length
and open him and climb in
and close him up after me, against the wind,
and sleep.

5
And dream
of lumbering flatfooted

over the tundra,
stabbed twice from within,
splattering a trail behind me,
splattering it out no matter which way I lurch,
no matter which parabola of bear-transcendence,
which dance of solitude I attempt,
which gravity-clutched leap,
which trudge, which groan.

6

Until one day I totter and fall —
fall on this
stomach that has tried so hard to keep up,
to digest the blood as it leaked in,
to break up
and digest the bone itself: and now the breeze
blows over me, blows off
the hideous belches of ill-digested bear blood
and rotted stomach
and the ordinary, wretched odor of bear,

blows across
my sore, lolled tongue a song
or screech, until I think I must rise up
and dance. And I lie still.

7

I awaken I think. Marshlights
reappear, geese
come trailing again up the flyway.
In her ravine under old snow the dam-bear
lies, licking
lumps of smeared fur
and drizzly eyes into shapes
with her tongue. And one
hairy-soled trudge stuck out before me,
the next groaned out,
the next,

the next,
the rest of my days I spend
wandering: wondering
what, anyway,
was that sticky infusion, that rank flavor of blood, that poetry, by which
    I lived?

MORTAL ACTS,
MORTAL WORDS

To Demetrio Delgado de Torres
tu valiente alegría

PART I

FERGUS FALLING

He climbed to the top
of one of those million white pines
set out across the emptying pastures
of the fifties — some program to enrich the rich
and rebuke the forefathers
who cleared it all once with ox and axe —
climbed to the top, probably to get out
of the shadow
not of those forefathers but of this father,
and saw for the first time,
down in its valley, Bruce Pond, giving off
its little steam in the afternoon,

pond where Clarence Akley came on Sunday mornings to cut down the
    cedars around the shore, I'd sometimes hear the slow spondees of
    his work, he's gone,
where Milton Norway came up behind me while I was fishing and stood
    awhile before I knew he was there, he's the one who put the cedar
    shingles on the house, some have curled or split, a few have blown
    off, he's gone,
where Gus Newland logged in the cold snap of '58, the only man will-
    ing to go into those woods that never got warmer than ten below,
    he's gone,
pond where two wards of the state wandered on Halloween, the Na-
    tional Guard searched for them in November, in vain, the next
    fall a hunter found their skeletons huddled together, in vain,
    they're gone,
pond where an old fisherman in a rowboat sits, drowning hooked
    worms, when he goes he's replaced and is never gone,

and when Fergus
saw the pond for the first time
in the clear evening, saw its oldness down there
in its old place in the valley, he became heavier suddenly
in his bones
the way fledglings do just before they fly,
and the soft pine cracked . . .

I would not have heard his cry
if my electric saw had been working,
its carbide teeth speeding through the bland spruce of our time, or
    burning
black arcs into some scavenged hemlock plank,
like dark circles under eyes
when the brain thinks too close to the skin,
but I was sawing by hand and I heard that cry
as though he were attacked; we ran out,
when we bent over him he said, "Galway, Inés, I saw a pond!"
His face went gray, his eyes fluttered closed a frightening moment . . .

Yes — a pond
that lets off its mist
on clear afternoons of August, in that valley
to which many have come, for their reasons,
from which many have gone, a few for their reasons, most not,
where even now an old fisherman only the pinetops can see
sits in the dry gray wood of his rowboat, waiting for pickerel.

AFTER MAKING LOVE
WE HEAR FOOTSTEPS

For I can snore like a bullhorn
or play loud music
or sit up talking with any reasonably sober Irishman
and Fergus will only sink deeper
into his dreamless sleep, which goes by all in one flash,
but let there be that heavy breathing
or a stifled come-cry anywhere in the house
and he will wrench himself awake
and make for it on the run — as now, we lie together,
after making love, quiet, touching along the length of our bodies,
familiar touch of the long-married,
and he appears — in his baseball pajamas, it happens,
the neck opening so small he has to screw them on —
and flops down between us and hugs us and snuggles himself to sleep,
his face gleaming with satisfaction at being this very child.

In the half darkness we look at each other
and smile
and touch arms across this little, startlingly muscled body —
this one whom habit of memory propels to the ground of his making,
sleeper only the mortal sounds can sing awake,
this blessing love gives again into our arms.

ANGLING, A DAY

Though day is just breaking
when we fling two nightcrawlers
bunched on a hook as far out
as we can into Crystal Lake so leaden
no living thing could possibly swim through it
and let them lie on the bottom, under the water
and mist in which the doubled sun
soon shines and before long the doubled
mountains; though we drag Lake Parker
with fishing apparatus of several sorts,
catching a few yellow perch which we keep
just to have caught *something*; though
we comb with fine, and also coarse,
toothed hooks Shirley's Pond stocked
with trout famous for swallowing
any sharpened wire no matter
how expertly disguised as worm;
though we fish the fish-prowled pools
Bill Allen has divined by dip of bamboo
during all those misspent days trout-witching
Miller Run; and then cast some hours
away at the Lamoille, at the bend
behind Eastern Magnesia Talc Company's
Mill No. 4, which Hayden Carruth
says his friend John Engels says
is the best fishing around ("hernia bend,"
Engels calls it, on account of the weight
of fish you haul out of there); and end up
fishing the Salmon Hole of the Winooski
in which twenty-inch walleyes moil —

we and a dozen others who keep faith
with earth by that little string
which ties each person to the river at twilight —
casting and, as we reel in, twitching the rod,
our bodies curvetting in that curious motion
by which people giving fish motions to lures
look themselves like fish, until Fergus' jig,
catching a rock as he reels in,
houdinies out of its knot, and the man
fishing next to us, Ralph, reeling
somewhat himself due to an afternoon
of no fish and much Molson's ale,
lends us one of his, and with shaking hands
ties a stout knot between line and jig,
while a fellow from downcountry
goes on about how to free a snagged line
by sliding a spark plug down it —
"Well," Ralph says a couple of times,
"I sure never heard of that one,"
though sure enough, a few minutes later,
when Ralph's own line gets snagged,
he takes the fellow up on the idea,
borrows the man's spark plug, taps
the gap closed over the line as directed,
and lets her slide, yanking and flapping
vigorously as the spark plug disappears
into the water, and instantly loses spark plug
and jig both, and says, "Nope,
I sure never heard of that one" —
though, in brief, we have crossed the entire state
up at its thick end, and fished with hope
all the above-mentioned fishing spots
from before first light to after nightfall
and now will just be able to make it
to Essex Junction in time
to wait the several hours that must pass
before the train arrives in reality,
we have caught nothing — not counting,

of course, the three yellow perch Fergus
gave away earlier to Bill and Anne
Allen's cat Monsoon, who is mostly dead
along her left side though OK on her right,
the side she was probably lying on the night
last winter when, literally, she half froze to death —
and being afraid that Fergus, who's so tired
he now gets to his feet only to cast
and at once sits down, might be thoroughly
defeated, and his noble passion for fishing
broken, I ask him how he feels:
"I'm disappointed," he says, "but not discouraged.
I'm not saying I'm a fisherman, but fishermen know
there are days when you don't catch anything."

SAINT FRANCIS AND THE SOW

The bud
stands for all things,
even for those things that don't flower,
for everything flowers, from within, of self-blessing;
though sometimes it is necessary
to reteach a thing its loveliness,
to put a hand on its brow
of the flower
and retell it in words and in touch
it is lovely
until it flowers again from within, of self-blessing;
as Saint Francis
put his hand on the creased forehead
of the sow, and told her in words and in touch
blessings of earth on the sow, and the sow
began remembering all down her thick length,
from the earthen snout all the way
through the fodder and slops to the spiritual curl of the tail,
from the hard spininess spiked out from the spine
down through the great broken heart
to the blue milken dreaminess spurting and shuddering
from the fourteen teats into the fourteen mouths sucking and blowing
    beneath them:
the long, perfect loveliness of sow.

THE CHOIR

Little beings with their hair blooming
so differently on skulls of odd sizes
and their eyes serious and their jaws
very firm from singing in Gilead, and with
their mouths gaping, saying
"Ah!" for God,
"O!" for an alphabet of O's,
they stand in rows, each as if suspended
from a fishing line
hooked at the breastbone, being hauled up
toward the heavenly gases.

Everyone who truly sings is beautiful.
Even sad music
requires absolute happiness:
eyes, nostrils, mouth strain together in quintal harmony
to sing Joy and Death well.

TWO SET OUT ON THEIR JOURNEY

We sit side by side,
brother and sister, and read
the book of what will be, while the wind
blows the pages over —
desolate odd, desolate even,
and otherwise. When it falls open
to our own story, the happy beginning,
the ending happy or not we don't know,
the ten thousand acts which encumber
and engross the days between,
we will read every page of it,
for if the ancestors have pressed
a love-flower for us, it will lie
between pages of the slow going,
where only those who adore the story
can find it. When it is time
to close the book and set out,
we will take the laughter of childhood
as far as we can into the days to come,
until we can hear, in the distance,
another laughter sounding back
from the earth where our next bodies
will have risen and will be laughing
at all that seemed deadly serious once,
offering to us new wayfarers
the light heart we started with,
now made of time and sorrow.

BROTHER OF MY HEART

for Etheridge Knight

Brother of my heart,
don't you know there's only one
walking into the light, only one,
before this light
flashes out, before this bravest knight
crashes his black bones into the earth?

You will not come back among us,
your cried-out face
laughing; because
those who die by the desire to die
maybe can love their way back,
but as moles or worms,
who grub into the first sorrow and lie there.

Therefore, as you are,
sing, even if you cry; the bravery
of the crying turns it into the true song; soul brother
in heaven, on earth
broken heart brother, sing to us
in this place that loses its brothers,
this emptiness the singing sometimes almost fills.

FISHERMAN

for Allen Planz

Solitary man, standing
on the Atlantic, high up on the floodtide
under the moon, hauling at nets
which shudder sideways under the mutilated darkness:
the one you hugged and slept with so often,
who hugged you and slept with you so often,
who has gone away now
into that imaginary moonlight of the greater world,
perhaps looks back at where you stand abandoned
on the floodtide, hauling at nets
and dragging from the darkness
anything, and feels tempted to walk over
and touch you
and speak
from that life to which she acquiesced suddenly dumbfounded,
but instead she only sings
in the sea-birds and breeze you imagine you remember but which you
    truly hear.

I don't know how you loved
or what marriage was and wasn't between you —
not even close friends understand anything of that —
but I know ordinary life was hard
and worry joined your brains' faces in pure, baffled lines
and therefore some deepest part of you has gone
with her, imprinted into her — imprinted now
into that world which only she doesn't fear any longer,
which you too will have ceased fearing —
and waits there to recognize you into it
after you've lived, lived past the sorrow,
if that happens, after all the time in the world.

WAIT

Wait, for now.
Distrust everything if you have to.
But trust the hours. Haven't they
carried you everywhere, up to now?
Personal events will become interesting again.
Hair will become interesting.
Pain will become interesting.
Buds that open out of season will become interesting.
Second-hand gloves will become lovely again;
their memories are what give them
the need for other hands. And the desolation
of lovers is the same: that enormous emptiness
carved out of such tiny beings as we are
asks to be filled; the need
for the new love *is* faithfulness to the old.

Wait.
Don't go too early.
You're tired. But everyone's tired.
But no one is tired enough.
Only wait a little and listen:
music of hair,
music of pain,
music of looms weaving all our loves again.
Be there to hear it, it will be the only time,
most of all to hear
the flute of your whole existence,
rehearsed by the sorrows, play itself into total exhaustion.

PART II

DAYBREAK

On the tidal mud, just before sunset,
dozens of starfishes
were creeping. It was
as though the mud were a sky
and enormous, imperfect stars
moved across it as slowly
as the actual stars cross heaven.
All at once they stopped,
and as if they had simply
increased their receptivity
to gravity they sank down
into the mud; faded down
into it and lay still; and by the time
pink of sunset broke across them
they were as invisible
as the true stars at daybreak.

THE GRAY HERON

It held its head still
while its body and green
legs wobbled in wide arcs
from side to side. When
it stalked out of sight,
I went after it, but all
I could find where I was
expecting to see the bird
was a three-foot-long lizard
in ill-fitting skin
and with linear mouth
expressive of the even temper
of the mineral kingdom.
It stopped and tilted its head,
which was much like
a fieldstone with an eye
in it, which was watching me
to see if I would go
or change into something else.

IN THE BAMBOO HUT

There would come to me the voices
of the washerwomen at the stream
where they threw dresses, shirts, pants,
into the green water, beat them,
wrung them out, arranged them empty
in our shapes on stones, murmuring,
laughing, sometimes one more forlorn
singing, a sound like that aftersinging
from those nights when we would sing
under the sign of the salamander
clinging to the wall above the bed,
motionless, attentive, bearing of desire.

LAVA

(The Hawaiian words — *pahoehoe*, *aa*, and *heiau* —
are pronounced pä·hō·ä·hō·ä; ä·ä; and hā·ē·ou.)

I want to be pahoehoe,
swirled, gracefully lined,
folded, frozen where I flowed,
a clear brazened surface
one can cross barefooted,
it's true; but even more,
I want to be aa,
a mass of rubble still
tumbling after I've stopped,
which a person without shoes
has to do deep knee-bends across,
groaning "aaaah! aaaah!" at each step,
or be heaped into a heiau
in sea-spray on an empty coast,
knowing in all my joints
the soft, crablice-ish clasp
of aa crumbling closer to aa.

When I approach the dismal shore
made, I know, of pahoehoe,
which is just hoi polloi of the slopes,
I don't want to call "ahoy! ahoy!"
and sail meekly in. Unh-unh.
I want to turn and look back
at that glittering, black aa
where we loved in the bright moon,
where our atoms broke and lived,
where even now two kneecaps gasp

"ah! ah!" to a heiau's stone floor,
to which the stone answers
"aaaaaah," in commiseration
with bones that find the way very long
and "aaaaaah" in envy of yet unbroken bones.

BLACKBERRY EATING

I love to go out in late September
among the fat, overripe, icy, black blackberries
to eat blackberries for breakfast,
the stalks very prickly, a penalty
they earn for knowing the black art
of blackberry making; and as I stand among them
lifting the stalks to my mouth, the ripest berries
fall almost unbidden to my tongue,
as words sometimes do, certain peculiar words
like *strengths* or *squinched* or *broughamed*,
many-lettered, one-syllabled lumps,
which I squeeze, squinch open, and splurge well
in the silent, startled, icy, black language
of blackberry eating in late September.

KISSING THE TOAD

Somewhere this dusk
a girl puckers her mouth
and considers kissing
the toad a boy has plucked
from the cornfield and hands
her with both hands;
rough and lichenous
but for the immense ivory belly,
like those old entrepreneurs
sprawling on Mediterranean beaches,
with popped eyes,
it watches the girl who might kiss it,
pisses, quakes, tries
to make its smile wider:
to love on, oh yes, to love on.

CRYING

Crying only a little bit
is no use. You must cry
until your pillow is soaked!
Then you can get up and laugh.
Then you can jump in the shower
and splash-splash-splash!
Then you can throw open your window
and, "Ha ha! ha ha!"
And if people say, "Hey,
what's going on up there?"
"Ha ha!" sing back, "Happiness
was hiding in the last tear!
I wept it! Ha ha!"

LES INVALIDES

At dusk by Les Invalides
a few old men play at boules,
tossing, holding
the crouch, listening for the clack
of steel on steel, strolling over, studying the ground.

At boules, it is the creaking grace, the slow amble, the stillness,
the dusk deepening,
the plane trees casting down their leaves,
the past blowing its shadows behind distracted eyes.

It is empty cots lined up
in the darkness of rooms where the last true men
listen each dusk
for the high, thin, sweet clack
sounding from the home village very far away.

ON THE TENNIS COURT AT NIGHT

We step out on the green rectangle
in moonlight; the lines glow,
which for many have been the only lines
of justice. We remember
the thousand trajectories the air has erased
of that close-contested last set —
blur of volleys, soft arcs of drop shots,
huge ingrown loops of lobs with topspin
which went running away, crosscourts recrossing
down to each sweet (and in exact proportion, bitter)
✪ in Talbert and Olds' *The Game of Doubles in Tennis.*
The breeze has carried them off but we still hear
the mutters, the doublefaulter's groans,
cries of "Deuce!" or "Love two!",
squeak of tennis shoes, grunt of overreaching,
all dozen extant tennis quips — "Just out!"
or, "About right for you?" or, "Want to change partners?"
and *baaah* of sheep translated very occasionally
into *thonk* of well-hit ball, among the pure
right angles and unhesitating lines
of this arena where every man grows old
pursuing that repertoire of perfect shots,
darkness already in his strokes,
even in death cramps waving an arm back and forth
to the disgust of the night nurse,
and smiling; and a few hours later found dead —
the smile still in place but the ice bag
she left on the brow now inexplicably
Scotchtaped to the right elbow — causing
all those bright trophies to slip permanently,

though not in fact much farther, out of reach,
all except the thick-bottomed young man
about to doublefault in soft metal on the windowsill:
"Runner-Up Men's Class B Consolation Doubles
St. Johnsbury Kiwanis Tennis Tournament 1969" . . .

Clouds come over the moon;
all the lines go out. November last year
in Lyndonville: it is getting dark,
snow starts falling, Zander Rubin wobble-twists
his worst serve out of the black woods behind him,
Stan Albro lobs into a gust of snow,
Don Bredes smashes at where the ball theoretically
could be coming down, the snow blows down
and swirls about our legs, darkness flows
across a disappearing patch of green-painted asphalt
in the north country, where four men,
half-volleying, poaching, missing, grunting,
begging mercy of their bones, hold their ground,
as winter comes on, all the winters to come.

PART III

THE SADNESS OF BROTHERS

1

He comes to me like a mouth
speaking from under several inches of water.
I can no longer understand what he is saying.
He has become one
who never belonged among us, someone
it is useless to think about or remember.

But this morning, I don't know why,
twenty-one years too late,
I imagine him back: his beauty
of feature wastreled down
to thick chin and wattles, his eyes
ratty, liver-lighted, he stands
at the door, and we face each other,
each of us knowing the lost brother.

2

I found a photograph
of a tractor ploughing a field — the ploughman
twisted in his iron seat
looking behind him at the turned-up earth — among
the photographs and drawings he hoarded up
of all the aircraft in the sky — Heinkel HE70s, Dewoitine D333
    "Antares," Loire-et-Olivier H24-2 —
and the fighting aircraft especially — Gloster Gauntlet, Fairey Battle I,
    Vickers Vildebeest Mark VII —
each shown crookedly
climbing an empty sky
the killer's blue of blue eyes

into which all his life he dreamed
he would fly; until pilot training, 1943,
when original fear
washed out
the flyingness in him; leaving
a man who only wandered
from then on, on roads
which ended twelve years later
in Wyoming, when he raced his big car
through the desert night, under
the Dipper
or Great Windshield Wiper
which, turning, squeegee-ed existence,
even in Wyoming, of its damaged dream life;
leaving only
old goods, few possessions,
matter which ceased to matter; and among the detritus,
the photographs of airplanes; and crawling
with negative force among these,
a tractor, in its iron
seat a farmer half turned, watching without expression
as the earth flattened away
into nowhere,
into the memory of a dead man's brother.

3
In this brother
I remember back, I see the father
I had so often seen in him . . . and known
in my own bones, too: the serene-
seeming, sea-going gait
which took him down Oswald Street in dark of each morning
and up Oswald Street in dark of each night . . .
this small, well-wandered Scotsman
who appears now in memory's memory,
in light of last days, jiggling
his knees as he used to do —
get out of here, I knew

they were telling him, *get out of here, Scotty* —
control he couldn't control
thwarting his desires down
into knees which could only jiggle
the one bit of advice least useful
to this man stuck in the ending-earth
of Pawtucket, Rhode Island; where his wife willed
the bourgeois illusion all of us dreamed
we lived, even he, who disgorged
divine capitalist law
out of his hungry craw,
though he had failed
at all its enterprises except war,
and perhaps war,
for what tales we eked from his reluctance
those Sunday mornings when six of us
hugged sideways in the double bed
revealed not much
of cowardice or courage: only medium mal
peered through pupils
screwed down very tiny, like a hunter's.

4

I think he's going to ask
for beer for breakfast, sooner
or later he'll start making obnoxious
remarks about race or sex
and criticize our loose ways
of raising children, while his eyes
grow more slick, his puritan heart more pure
by virtue of sins sinned
against the mother, who used to sit up
crying for the lost Ireland
of no American sons,
no pimpled, surly fourteen-year-olds
who would slip out at night, blackjack
in pocket, .22 pistol in homemade armpit holster,
to make out with rich men's wives

at the Narragansett Track now vanished,
on the back stretch of which horses ran
down the runway of the even more obliterated
What Cheer Airport, where a Waco biplane
flew up for a joyride in 1931
with him waving from the rear cockpit,
metamorphosed at age six;
and who would stagger home
near dawn, snarl to reproaches, silence to tears.

5

But no, that's fear's reading.
We embrace in the doorway,
in the frailty of large,
fifty-odd-year-old bodies
of brothers only one of whom has imagined
those we love, who go away,
among them this brother,
stopping suddenly
as a feeling comes over them
that just now we remember
and miss them, and then turning
as though to make their own
even more vivid memories
known across to us — if it's true,
of love, only what
the flesh can bear surrenders to time.

Past all that, we stand
in the memory that came to me this day
of a man twenty-one years strange to me,
tired, vulnerable, half the world old; and in large,
fat-gathering bodies, with sore, well or badly spent,
but spent, hearts, we hold each other, friends to reality,
knowing the ordinary sadness of brothers.

GOODBYE

1

My mother, poor woman, lies tonight
in her last bed. It's snowing, for her, in her darkness.
I swallow down the goodbyes I won't get to use,
tasteless, with wretched mouth-water;
whatever we are, she and I, we're nearly cured.

The night years ago when I walked away
from that final class of junior high school students
in Pittsburgh, the youngest of them ran
after me down the dark street. "Goodbye!" she called,
snow swirling across her face, tears falling.

2

Tears have kept on falling. History
has taught them its slanted understanding
of the human face. At each last embrace the dying give,
the snow brings down its disintegrating curtain.
The mind shreds the present, once the past is over.

In the Derry graveyard where only her longings sleep
and armfuls of flowers go out in the drizzle
the bodies not yet risen must lie nearly forever . . .
"Sprouting good Irish grass," the graveskeeper blarneys,
he can't help it, "a sprig of shamrock, if they were young."

3

In Pittsburgh tonight, those who were young
will be less young, those who were old, more old, or more likely
no more; and the street where Syllest,

fleetest of my darlings, caught up with me
and hugged me and said goodbye, will be empty. Well,

one day the streets all over the world will be empty —
already in heaven, listen, the golden cobblestones have fallen still —
everyone's arms will be empty, everyone's mouth, the Derry earth.
It is written in our hearts, the emptiness is all.
That is how we have learned, the embrace is all.

LOOKING AT YOUR FACE

Looking at your face
now you have become ready to die
is like kneeling at an old gravestone
on an afternoon with no sun, trying to read
the white chiselings of the poem
in the white stone.

THE LAST HIDING PLACES OF SNOW

1

The burnt tongue
fluttered, "I'm dying . . ."
and then, "Why did . . . ? Why . . . ?"
What earthly knowledge did she still need
just then, when
the tongue failed
or began speaking in another direction?

Only the struggle for breath
remained: groans made
of all the goodbyes ever spoken all
turned meaningless; surplus world sucked back
into a body laboring to live
all the way to death; and past death, if it must.

There is a place in the woods
where you can hear
such sounds: sighs, groans
seeming to come
from the darkness of spruce boughs,
from glimmer-at-night of the white birches,
from the last hiding places of snow,

a breeze,
that's all, driving
across certain obstructions: every stump
speaks,
the spruce needles play out of the air
the sorrows cried into it somewhere else.

Once in a while, passing the place,
I have imagined I heard
my old mother calling, thinking out loud her
mother-love toward me, over those many miles
from where her bones lie,
five years
in earth now, with my father's thirty-years' bones.

I have always felt
anointed by her love, its light
like sunlight
falling through broken panes
onto the floor
of a deserted house: we may go, it remains,
telling of goodness of being, of permanence.

So lighted I have believed
I could wander anywhere,
among any foulnesses, any contagions,
I could climb through the entire empty world
and find my way back and learn again to be happy.

But when I've stopped and listened,
all I've heard was
what may once have been speech
or groans, now
sieved to a hiss from passing
through a valley of spruce needles.

My mother did not want me to be born;
afterwards, all her life, she needed me to return.
When this more-than-love flowed toward me, it brought darkness;
as if she wanted me as burial earth wants — to heap itself gently upon
        but also to annihilate —
and I knew, whenever I felt longings to go back,
that must be what wanting to die is.

2

I was not at her bedside
that final day, I did not grant her ancient,
huge-knuckled hand
its last wish, I did not let it
gradually become empty of the son's hand — and so
hand her, with more steadiness, into the future.
Instead, old age took her
by force, though with the help
of her old, broken attachments
which had broken
only on this side of death
but had kept intact on the other.

I would know myself lucky if my own children
could be at my deathbed, to take
my hand in theirs and with theirs
to bless some part of me back into the world,
with smoothness pressed into roughness,
with folding-light fresh runner hands to runner of wasted breath,
with mortal touch whose mercy two bundled-up figures greeting on a
     freezing morning, exposing the ribboned ends of right arms, en-
     twining these, squeeze back and forth before walking on,
with memories these hands keep, of strolling down Bethune Street in
     spring, a little creature hanging from each arm, by a hand so small
     it can do no more than press its tiny thumb into the soft beneath
     my thumb . . .

But for my own mother I was not there . . .
and at the gates of the world, therefore, between
holy ground
and ground of almost all its holiness gone, I loiter
in stupid fantasies I can live that day again.

Why did you come so late?
Why will you go too early?

I know there are regrets
we can never be rid of;
permanent remorse. I know also
I am to draw from that surplus stored up
of tenderness which was hers by right,
which no one ever gave her,
and give it away, freely.

3
A child, a little girl,

in violet hat, blue scarf, green sweater, yellow skirt, orange socks, red
    boots,
on a rope swing, swings
in sunlight
over a garden in Ireland, backfalls,
backrises,
forthsinks,
forthsoars, her charmed life holding its breath
innocent of groans, beyond any
future, far past the past: into a pure present.

Now she wears rhythmically into the air
of morning
the rainbow's curve, but upside down
so that angels may see
beloved dross promising heaven:
no matter what fire we invent to destroy us,
ours will have been the brightest world ever existing . . .

Every so often, when I look
at the dark sky, I know she remains
among the old endless blue lightedness
of stars; or finding myself out in a field
in November, when a strange
starry perhaps first snowfall blows
down across the darkening air, lightly,
I know she is there, where snow

falls flakes down fragile softly
falling until I can't see the world
any longer, only its stilled shapes.

Even now when I wake at night
in some room far from everyone,
the darkness sometimes
lightens a little, and then,
because of nothing,
in spite of nothing,
in an imaginary daybreak, I see her,
and for that moment I am still her son
and I am in the holy land
and twice in the holy land, remembered
within her, and remembered in the memory
her old body slowly executes into the earth.

52 OSWALD STREET

for Wendy Plummer and Jill Niekamp

Then, when the full moonlight
would touch our sleeping bodies,
we liked to think it filled
us with what we imagined was
fullness — actual bright matter
drifted down from the moon's
regions, so that when we woke
we would be shining. Now,
wherever we are on earth,
in loneliness, or loneliness-
easing arms, by whatever means
stricken awake, dream, regret,
our own grunt rebounding back
from the appalled future, we three
who have survived the lives
and deaths in the old house
on Oswald Street can almost
feel that full moonlight again,
as someone might hear the slow-
given sighs of post-coital bliss
the lover who ran off could be
breathing this minute in someone
else's arms; and we taste
the lost fullness and we know how
far our hearts have crumbled, how
our feelings too long attuned
to having couldn't bear up, that for us
three gravesides were too many
to stand at, or turn from,
that most mired of pivotings,

and our mouths fill with three
names that have lost their meanings,
theirs, and before we know it, also
ours, and we pull up more tightly
around us the blanket of full
moonlight which falls down
now from unrepeatable life
on bodies of mother and father
and three children, and a fourth,
sleeping, quite long ago.

PART IV

THE RAINBOW

The rainbow appears above us
for its minute, then vanishes, as though
we had wished it, making us
turn more carefully to what we can
touch and feel, things and creatures
we know we haven't dreamed: flutings
on a match stick, the small,
blurry warmth a match gives back
to thumb and forefinger
when we hold it into the spewing
gas, for instance, or
the pelvic bones of a woman
lying on her back, which rise
smoothed by ten thousand years
on either side of the crater
we floated in, in the first life,
that last time we knew
more of happiness than of time,
before the world-ending inkling
of what pain would be for all
of our natural going — a blow so well-struck
space simply breaks — befell us,
and we fell, scanning about,
the cleverest of us, for a lover
to cling to, and howling
howls of the damned so fierce
they put terrified grooves
permanently into the throat,
which can't relax ever again,
until the day the carcass expels

defeated desire in one final curve
of groaning breath, the arc
farewelling hands have polished
before each face, a last outrush
which rises through the iridescence
of spent tears, across a momentarily
heavenly sky, then dies
toward those invisible fires,
the other, unfulfilled galaxies,
to win them over, too, into time and ruin.

THE APPLE

1

The brain
cringes around the worst
that it knows; just as the apple
must have, when those two
bit into it, poisoning themselves
into the joy
that has to watch itself go away.

No one easily
survives love; neither the love
one has, nor the love
one has not; each breaks down
in the red smoke blown up
of the day when all love will have gone on.

A little sadness,
a little more self-cruelty,
a little more uselessness. These won't last.

What will last is that
no one knows enough
to let go, everyone still needs to know
the one he or she doesn't know
all the way to the end of the world.

2

When lovers embrace,
sometimes their arms seem only
to be remembering the other; their heads

become heavier
with ancient understandings, that skulls shall be
moonstones
and lie broken open
under the moon, only an icy light thinking inside them,
on grass
which long ago gave its stitchmarks away
to the bodies of lovers
who exist only
as leaves do, that have rotted back into the apple
still brightening its bitter knowledge above us
which needs to be tasted without fear
to be the philosophers' stone of the risen world.

MEMORY OF WILMINGTON

Thirty-some years ago, hitchhiking
north on Route 1, I stopped for the night
at Wilmington, Delaware, one of those American cities
that start falling apart before they ever get finished.
I met, I remember, an ancient hobo — I almost remember
his name — at the ferry — now dead,
of course, him,
and also the ferry —
in great-brimmed hat, coat to his knees,
pants dragging the ground, semi-zootish rig
plucked off various clotheslines.

He taught me how to grab a hen
so the dogs won't hear: how to come up on it
from behind, swoop down and swing it up
and whirl it, all in one motion,
breaking the neck, of course, also twisting
silent any cry
for help it might want to utter.

It doesn't matter.
It doesn't matter
that we ill-roasted our hen over brushwood
or that with the squeamishness
of the young I dismouthed the rawest of it
the fire hadn't so much as warmed and tossed it
behind me into the black waters of Delaware Bay.

After he ate, the old hobo
— *Amos!* yes, that was his name! — old Amos sang,

or rather laughed forth a song or two, his voice
creaking out slower and slower,
like the music in old music boxes, when time slows itself down in them.
I sat in the last light and listened, there among rocks,
tin cans, feathers, ashes, old stars. This. This.

The next morning the sun was out
when I sailed north on the ferry.
From the rotting landing Amos waved.
I was fifteen, I think. Wilmington then
was far along on its way to becoming a city
and already well advanced on its way back to dust.

THE STILL TIME

I know there is still time —
time for the hands
to open,
to be filled
by those failed harvests,
the imagined bread of the days of not having.

I remember those summer nights
when I was young and empty,
when I lay through the darkness
wanting, wanting,
knowing
I would have nothing of anything I wanted —
that total craving
that hollows the heart out irreversibly.

So it surprises me now to hear
the steps of my life following me —
so much of it gone
it returns, everything that drove me crazy
comes back, as if blessing the misery
of each step it took me into the world;
as though a prayer had ended
and the changed
air between the palms goes free
to become the glitter
on common things that inexplicably shine.

And the old voices,
which once made broken-off, choked, parrot-incoherences,

speak again,
this time on the palatum cordis,
saying there is still time
for those who can groan
to sing,
for those who can sing to heal themselves.

THERE ARE THINGS I TELL TO NO ONE

1

There are things I tell to no one.
Those close to me might think
I was sad, and try to comfort me, or become sad themselves.
At such times I go off alone, in silence, as if listening for God.

2

I say "God"; I believe,
rather, in a music of grace
that we hear, sometimes, playing
from the other side of happiness.
When we hear it and it flows
through our bodies, it lets us live
these days intensified by their vanity
worshipping, as the other animals do,
who live and die in the spirit
of the end, that backward-spreading
brightness. And it speaks in notes struck
or caressed or blown or plucked
off our own bodies: *remember*
existence already remembers
the flush upon it you will have been,
you who have reached out ahead
and taken up some of the silvery dust
we become, souvenir
which was already glittering in your hand.

3

Just as the supreme cry
of joy, the cry of orgasm, also has a ghastliness to it,
as though it touched forward

into the chaos where we break apart, so the death-groan
sounding into us from another direction carries us back
to our first world, so that the one
whose mouth acids up with it remembers
how oddly fearless he felt
at first imagining the dead,
at first seeing the grandmother or grandfather sitting only yesterday
on the once cluttered, now sadly tidy porch,
that little boned body drowsing almost unobserved into the agreement
    to die.

4

Brothers and sisters;
lovers and children;
great mothers and grand fathers
whose love-times have been cut
already into stone; great
grand fœtuses spelling
the past again into the flesh's waters:
can you bless — or not curse —
whatever struggles to stay alive
on this planet of struggles?
The nagleria eating the convolutions
from the black pulp of thought,
or the spirochete rotting down
the last temples of Eros, the last god?

Then the last cry in the throat
or only dreamed into it
by its threads too wasted to cry
will be but an ardent note
of gratefulness so intense
it disappears into that music
which carries our time on earth away
on the catafalque
of spine marrowed with god's-flesh,
thighs bruised by the blue flower,
pelvis that makes angels shiver to know down here we mortals make
    love with our bones.

I want to live forever.
I am like everyone. But when I hear
coming through the walls
those grace-notes blown
out of the wormed-out bones,
music that their memory of blood
plucks from the straitened arteries,
that the hard cock and soaked cunt
caressed from each other
in the holy days of their vanity,
that the two hearts drummed
out of their ribs together,
the hearts that know everything (and even
the little knowledge they can leave
stays, to be the light of this house),

then it is not so difficult
to go out, to turn and face
the spaces which gather into one sound the singing
of mortal lives, waves of spent existence
which flow toward, and toward, and on which we flow
and grow drowsy and become fearless again.

PONT NEUF AT NIGHTFALL

Just now a sprinkling
of rain begins. It brings with it
an impression of more lasting existence —
brings it by removal, by the swiftness
of each drop's drying from the stone.
(Soon the stone will be completely wet.
When *our* stone became wet, that was
when desolation came into the world.)
We can't grasp our full debt
to the old masters who heaped up
these stones into palaces,
arches, spires, into a grace
which, being behind us, is beyond us.
But we pay them some envy, we imagine
a memory filled almost completely
with what is, without room
for longing backward; and also
some sadness, sadness which
comes back and tries to restore us,
being the knowledge that happiness
is not here but
that it exists, even if out of reach.
A girl walks by, a presence
in someone's memory, and she is
smiling, clasping flowers
and trailing their odor and the memory
of her into the brief past
which follows closely behind.
A light comes on very dim in a hotel
window, like a glint of what once was

the light of the world. In that tiny room
overlooking a bridge and a dark river, that would be
where it could come on:
over a narrow bed where a girl and a boy
give themselves into time and memory.

THE APPLE TREE

I remember this tree,
its white flowers all unfallen.
It's the fall, the unfallen apples
hold their brightness
a little longer into the blue air, hold the idea
that they can be brighter.

We create without turning,
without looking back, without ever
really knowing we create.
Having tasted
the first flower of the first spring
we go on,
we don't turn again
until we touch the last flower of the last spring.

And that day, fondling
each grain one more time, like the overturned hourglass,
we die
of the return-streaming of everything we have lived.

When the fallen apple rolls
into the grass, the apple worm
stops, then goes
all the way through and looks out
at the creation unopposed, the world
made entirely of lovers.

Or else there is no such thing as memory,
or else there are only the empty branches,

only the blossoms upon them,
only the apples,
that still grow full,
that still fail into brightness,
that still invent past their own decay the dream
they can be brighter,
that still
that still

The one who holds still and looks out,
alone
of all of us, that one may die mostly of happiness.

THE MILK BOTTLE

A tiny creature moves
through the tide pool, holding up
its little fortress foretelling
our tragedies; another clamps
itself down to the stone. A sea anemone
sucks at my finger, mildly, I can just
feel it, though it may mean to kill — no,
it would probably say, to eat
and flow, for all these creatures
even half made of stone seem to thrill
to altered existences. As do we ourselves,
who advance so far, then stop, then creep
a little, stop again, suddenly gasp — breath
is the bright shell
of our life-wish encasing us — gasp
it all back in, on seeing that any time
would be OK
to go, to vanish back into all things — as when
lovers wake up at night and see
the other is crying and think, *Yes,*
but it doesn't matter, already
we will have lived forever. And yes,
if we could do that: separate out
the molecules, scattered
throughout our flesh, that remember, skim them off,
give them to non-conscious things,
who may even crave them . . . It's funny,
I imagine I can actually remember one certain
quart of milk which has just finished clinking
against its brethren

in the milkman's hand and stands,
freeing itself from itself, on the rotting
doorstep in Pawtucket in 1932,
which is picked up and taken inside
by one in whom time hasn't yet completely
woven all its tangles, and is not ever set down . . .
So that here, by the tide pool,
where a sea eagle rings its glass voice
above us, I remember myself back there,
and first dreams easily untangling
themselves rise in me, flow from me,
as if they felt ready now to be fulfilled
out there where there is nothing.
The old bottle will shatter of its own
high clink, the sea eagle
cry itself back down into the sea
the sea's creatures transfigure over and over.
Look. Everything has changed.
Ahead of us the meantime is overflowing.
Around us its own almost-invisibility
streams and sparkles over everything.

FLYING HOME

1

It is good for strangers
of few nights to love each other
(as she and I did, eighteen years ago,
strangers of a single night)
and merge in natural rapture —
though it isn't exactly *each other*
but through each other some
force in existence they don't acknowledge
yet propitiate, no matter where,
in the least faithful of beds,
and by the quick dopplering of horns
of trucks plunging down Delancey,
and next to the iron rumblings
of outlived technology, subways up for air,
which blunder past every ten minutes
and botch the TV screen in the next apartment,
where the man in his beer
has to get up from his chair over and over
to soothe the bewildered jerking
things dance with internally,
and under the dead-light of neon,
and among the mating of cockroaches,
and *like* the mating of cockroaches
who were etched before the daybreak
of the gods with compulsions to repeat
that drive them, too, to union
by starlight, without will or choice.

It is also good — and harder —
for lovers who live many years together

to feel their way toward
the one they know completely
and don't ever quite know,
and to be with each other
and to increase what light may shine
in their ashes and let it go out
toward the other, and to need
the whole presence of the other
so badly that the two together
wrench their souls from the future
in which each mostly wanders alone
and in this familiar-strange room,
for this night which lives
amid daily life past and to come
and lights it, find they hold,
perhaps shimmering a little,
or perhaps almost spectral, only the loved
other in their arms.

2

Flying home, looking about
in this swollen airplane, every seat
of it squashed full with one of us,
it occurs to me I might be the luckiest
in this planeload of the species;

for earlier,
in the airport men's room, seeing
the middleaged men my age,
as they washed their hands after touching
their penises — when it might have been more in accord
with the lost order to wash first, then touch —
peer into the mirror
and then stand back, as if asking, who is this?

I could only think
that one looks relieved to be getting away,
that one dreads going where he goes;

while as for me, at the very same moment
I feel regret at leaving
and happiness to be flying home.

3

As this plane dragging
its track of used ozone half the world long
thrusts some four hundred of us
toward places where actual known people
live and may wait,
we diminish down into our seats,
disappeared into novels of lives clearer than ours,
and yet we do not forget for a moment
the life down there, the doorway each will soon enter:
where I will meet her again
and know her again,
dark radiance with, and then mostly without, the stars.

Very likely she has always understood
what I have slowly learned
and which only now, after being away, almost as far away
as one can get on this globe, almost
as far as thoughts can carry — yet still in her presence,
still surrounded not so much by reminders of her
as by things she had already reminded me of,
shadows of her
cast forward and waiting — can I try to express:

that while many good things are easy, love is hard,
because it is first of all a power,
its own power,
and must keep making its way forward, from night
into day, from transcending union forward into difficult day.

And as the plane starts its descent, it comes to me,
up here in the space where tears stream across the stars
before they are shed on the actual earth
where their shining is what we call spirit,

that once the lover
recognizes the other, knows for the first time
what is most to be valued in another,
from then on, love is very much like courage,
perhaps it *is* courage, and even
perhaps
only courage. Squashed
out of old selves, smearing the darkness
of expectation across experience, all of us little
thinkers it brings home having similar thoughts
of landing to the imponderable world,
the transcontinental airliner,
resisting its huge weight down, comes in almost lightly,
to where
with sudden, tiny, white puffs and long, black, rubberish smears
all its tires *know* the home ground.

THE PAST

FOR INÉS

PART I

THE ROAD BETWEEN HERE AND THERE

Here I heard the snorting of hogs trying to re-enter the underearth.

Here I came into the curve too fast, on ice, and touched the brake and sailed into the pasture.

Here I stopped the car and snoozed while two small children crawled all over me.

Here I reread *Moby Dick*, skimming big chunks, in a single day, while Maud and Fergus fished.

Here I abandoned the car because of a clonk in the motor and hitchhiked (which in those days in Vermont meant walking the whole way with a limp) all the way to a garage where I passed the afternoon with ex-loggers who had stopped by to oil the joints of their artificial limbs and talk.

Here a barn burned down to the snow. "Friction," one of the ex-loggers said. "Friction?" "Yup, the mortgage, rubbing against the insurance policy."

Here I went eighty but was in no danger of arrest, for I was "blessed speeding" — trying to get home in time to see my children before they slept.

Here I bought speckled brown eggs with bits of straw shitted to them.

Here I brought home in the back seat two piglets who rummaged inside the burlap sack like pregnancy itself.

Here I heard on the car radio Handel's concerto for harp and lute, for the second time in my life, which Inés played to me the first time, making me want to drive after it and hear it forever.

Here I sat on a boulder by the winter-steaming river and put my head in my hands and considered time — which is next to nothing, merely what vanishes, and yet can make one's elbows nearly pierce one's thighs.

Here I forgot how to sing in the old way and listened to frogs at dusk.

Here the local fortune teller took my hand and said, "What is still possible is inspired work, faithfulness to a few, and a last love,

which, being last, will be like looking up and seeing the parachute
dissolving in a shower of bright light."
Here is the chimney standing up by itself and falling down, which tells
you you approach the end of the road between here and there.
Here I arrive there.
And I must turn around and go back and on the way back look to left
and to right and look for any spaces not yet used up.

THE ANGEL

This angel, who mediates between us
and the world underneath us, trots ahead
so cheerfully. Now and then she bends
her spine down hard, like a dowser's branch,
over some, to her, well-known splashing spot
of holy water, of which she herself in turn
carefully besoms out a thrifty sprinkle.
Trotting ahead again, she scribbles her spine's
continuation into immaterial et cetera,
thus signaling that it is safe for us now
to go wagging our legs along vertically as we do,
across the ups and downs under which lie
ancestors dog-toothed millennia ago into oblivion.
Tonight she will crouch at the hearth,
where demons' breaths flutter up among the logs,
gnawing a freshly unearthed bone — bone of a dog,
if possible — making logs and bone together
cry through the room, *crack splinter groan*.

MIDDLE OF THE NIGHT

A telephone rings through the wall.
Nobody answers. Exactly how
the mouth shapes itself inside
saying the word "gold" is what sleep
would be like if one were happy.
So Kenny Hardman and George Sykes
called "Gaw-way-ay!" at the back
of the house. If I didn't come out
they would call until nightfall,
like summer insects. Or like
the pay phone at the abandoned
filling station, which sometimes
rang, off and on, an entire day.
The final yawn before one sleeps
is the word "yes" said too many times,
too rapidly. On the landing
she turned and looked back. Something
of the sea turtle heavy with eggs,
looking back at the sea. The shocking dark
of her eyes awakened in me
the affirmative fire. It would have hurt
to walk away, just as it would bewilder
a mouth making the last yawn to say "no."

CONCEPTION

Having crowed the seed
of the child of his heart
into the egg of the child
of her heart in the dark middle
of the night, as cocks
sometimes cry out to a light
not yet visible to the rest,
and lying there with cock
shrugging its way out of her,
and rising back through phases
of identity, he hears
her say, "Yes, I am two now,
and with you, three."

THE SOW PIGLET'S ESCAPES

When the little sow piglet squirmed free,
Gus and I ran her all the way down to the swamp
and lunged and floundered and fell full-length
on our bellies stretching for her — and got her! —
and lay there, all three shining with swamp slime —
she yelping, I laughing, Gus — it was then I knew
he would die soon — gasping and gasping.
She made her second escape on the one day
she was just big enough to dig an escape hole
and still small enough to squeeze through it.
Every day for the next week I took a bucket of meal
to her plot of rooted-up ground in the woods,
until one day there she was, waiting for me,
the wild beast evidently all mealed out of her.
She trotted over and let me stroke her back
and, dribbling corn down her chin, put up her little worried face
as if to remind me not to forget to recapture her —
though, really, a pig's special alertness to death
ought to have told her: in Sheffield the *dolce vita*
leads to the Lyndonville butcher. When I seized her
she wriggled hard and cried, *wee wee wee*, all the way home.

THE OLIVE WOOD FIRE

When Fergus woke crying at night
I would carry him from his crib
to the rocking chair and sit holding him
before the fire of thousand-year-old olive wood.
Sometimes, for reasons I never knew and
he has forgotten, even after his bottle the big tears
would keep on rolling down his big cheeks
— the left cheek always more brilliant than the right —
and we would sit, some nights for hours,
rocking in the almost lightless light
eking itself out of the ancient wood,
and hold each other against the darkness,
his close behind and far away in the future,
mine I imagined all around.
One such time, fallen half-asleep myself,
I thought I heard a scream
— a flier crying out in horror
as he dropped fire on he didn't know what or whom,
or else a child thus set aflame —
and sat up alert. The olive wood fire
had burned low. In my arms lay Fergus,
fast asleep, left cheek glowing, God.

MILK

When he pulls back on the oars
slightly too large for him, the boat
surges forward, toward the island
where he picks up the milk bottle
the old man he's never seen
puts out at the end of the dock;
toward the shore by the highway
where he exchanges four empty
milk bottles for the four full
the milkman he's never seen either
sets down to glow at roadside;
toward the dock where he leaves
one full bottle for the old man;
toward home across lake water
around which the shore trees stand
right side up in the world
and upside down in the world under it,
into which utterly still moments
are the doors childhood almost opens,
bringing back milk in time for breakfast.

LAKE MEMPHREMAGOG

We loaf in our gray boat in the sunshine.
The Canadian Pacific freight following the shoreline sends a racket of
    iron over Lake Memphremagog.
The children cast, the fishes do not bite.
They leap into the water and splash, the Memphremagog monster does
    not bite.
Far off, in the center of Newport, the train blows, one after one, all its
    five horns.
Long ago I astonished my own cheeks with the amount of fluid one
    child can cry.
Those nights now lie almost farther away than memory goes.
All the elsewheres, so far away, as the train's cries fade, fade.
Our boat lies very still in the Memphremagog water, and it's still.
Here everybody is OK.
I am fifty. The children are just little ones.

THE MAN SPLITTING WOOD
IN THE DAYBREAK

The man splitting wood in the daybreak
looks strong, as though, if one weakened,
one could turn to him and he would help.
Gus Newland was strong. When he split wood
he struck hard, flashing the bright steel
through air of daybreak so fast rock maple
leapt apart — as they think marriages will
in countries about to institute divorce —
and even willow, which, though stacked
to dry a full year, on separating
actually weeps — totem wood, therefore,
to the married-until-death — sunders
with many little lip-wetting gasps.
But Gus is dead. We could turn to our fathers,
but they protect us only through the unperplexed
looking-back of the numerals cut into headstones.
Or to our mothers, whose love, so devastated,
can't, even in spring, break through the hard earth.
Our spouses weaken at the same rate we do.
We have to hold our children up to lean on them.
Everyone who could help goes or hasn't arrived.
What about the man splitting wood in the daybreak,
who looked strong? That was years ago. That man was me.

THE FROG POND

In those first years I came down
often to the frog pond — formerly,
before the earthen dam wore away,
the farm pond — to bathe, standing
on a rock and throwing pond water over me,
and doing it quickly because of the leeches,
who need but minutes to know you're there,
or to read the mail or to scribble
or to loaf and think — sometimes of the future —
while the one deer fly
that torments everyone who walks in July
in Vermont — smack it dead as often
as one will — buzzed about my head.
A few years after I got here,
the beavers came, the waters rose,
and the frog pond became the beaver pond.
The next year an old rowboat surfaced,
with sheet metal nailed all around it
to hold the hull boards in place
while they rotted. The four
of us would oar, pole, and bale out
a few feet above the sunken green bank
where a man used to sit and think
and look up and seem to see four people
up here oaring and poling and baling out
above him: the man *seems* happy,
the two children laugh and splash,
a slight shadow crosses the woman's face.
Then one spring the beavers disappeared —
trapped off, or else gone away

on their own to make a pond elsewhere —
in which case this pond and that one
and the next, one after one, will flow off,
each leaving behind its print
in the woods, a sudden green meadow
with gleams of sky meandering through it.
The man who lies propped up
on an elbow, scribbling in a notebook
or loafing and thinking, will be older
and will remember this place held a pond once,
writhing with leeches and overflown
by the straight blue bodies of dragonflies,
and will think of small children
grown up and of true love broken
and will sit up abruptly and swat
the hard-biting deer fly on his head,
crushing it into his hair, as he has done before.

THE OLD LIFE

The waves collapsed into themselves
with heavy rumbles in the darkness
and the soprano shingle whistled
gravely its way back into the sea.
When the moon came from behind clouds
its white full-moon's light
lightly oiled the little beach stones
back into silence. We stood
among shatterings, glitterings,
the brilliance. For some reason
to love does not seem ever
to hurt any less. Now it happens
another lifetime is up for us,
another life is upon us.
What's left is what is left
of the whole absolutely love-time.

PART II

PRAYER

Whatever happens. Whatever
what is is is what
I want. Only
that. But that.

THE FERRY STOPPING AT MACMAHON'S POINT

It comes vigorously in,
nudges the jetty and ties up,
the usually ill-tossed line tossed twice,
presses by engine pressure against
the pilings for about a half-minute,
backs out, turns, and prow lifted
like the head of a swimming dog,
makes for the Lavender Bay jetty.

MOUNT FUJI AT DAYBREAK

From the Fuji-view stand made of cinder block
a crow watches Fuji rise into daybreak.
Trash smoke light-blues the exhausted valley.
Hot-spring steam blows up out of steam holes.
Up the road out of town a tanker truck groans.
An electric bullhorn now crackles messages
to workers coming early out of their doors.
From the cinder block Fuji-view stand the crow
flies off repeating the round vowel "ah!"
to Mount Fuji now risen bright into daybreak,
or else, "ha! ha! ha! ha!"

BREAK OF DAY

He turns the light on, lights
the cigarette, goes out on the porch,
chainsaws a block of green wood down the grain,
puts the pieces into the box stove,
pours in kerosene, tosses in the match
he set fire to the next cigarette with,
stands back while the creosote-lined, sheet-
metal rust-lengths shudder but manage
to lure the *cawhoosh* from inside the stove,
which sucks in ash motes through holes at the bottom
and glares out fire blaze through cracks around the top,
all the way to the roof and up out through
into the still starry sky starting to fade,
sits down to a bowl of crackers and blue milk
in which reflections of a 40-watt ceiling bulb
try to drown, eats, contemplates
an atmosphere containing kerosene stink,
chainsaw smoke, chainsmoke, wood smoke, wood heat,
gleams of a 40-watt ceiling bulb in blue milk.

FARM PICTURE

Black earth
turned up, clods
shining on their
western sides, hay
sprouting on top
of bales of spoiled
hay, an old
farmer bent far
over like *Australopithecus
robustus*, carrying two dented
pails of water out
to the hen yard.

SOME SONG

On a stoop
the old man
is drinking him
some beer,
the boy in
his yellow shirt
is playing
him some banjo tune,
the old fellow
hasn't any
teeth, and the boy
sings him
some song.

COINALISTE

She can drink from a beer bottle.
She can light a cigar and sneeze out the match.
She can drag on it so hard the end blazes.
She can inhale without coughing.
She can blow a smoke ring or two.
She can withdraw and introspect.

She can play the nose flute: f̄# with lower hole unstopped; ā̄ with both
    holes unstopped; c̄̄# with both stopped: the tonic, the mediant,
    the dominant of the chord of F# major.
She can suck the whole instrument inside, where it continues to sing
    and cry.
She can speak a pouting, pidgin blabber.

She can clench on the ictus and moan on the arsis but can't come on
    the thesis.
She can wink and throw French kisses.
She can motherly-kiss the fuzzy cheeks of young sailors.
She can pick up the money they toss, including the dollar bills.
She can count but not give change.
She can smile.

DRIFTWOOD FROM A SHIP

It is the white of faces from which the sunburn has suddenly been
scared away.

It has the rounded shoulders of those who fear they will pass the rest of
their days alone.

The final moments of one it couldn't hold up — possibly the cook, who
possibly could neither cook nor swim — have been gasped into it.

The black residue inside the black holes — three set close together,
three far apart, three close — remembers nine nails hammered
into their vanishing places.

A plane's long, misericording *shhhhhhhhh*'s long ago soothed away the
halo segments the sawmill's circular saw had tormented across its
planes.

The pebbles it rubs itself into fuzz up all over it a first beard, white right
from the start.

Its grain cherishes the predicament of spruce, which has a trunk that
rises and boughs that fall.

Its destiny is to disappear.

This could be accomplished when a beachcomber extracts its heat and
resolves the rest into smoke and ashes; or in the normal way,
through irritation and evanescence.

FIRE IN LUNA PARK

The screaming produced by the great fright machines —
one like a dough beater that lifts, turns, plunges the victims strapped to
    its arms,
one a huge fluted pan that tries to whirl its passengers off the earth,
one that holds its riders upside down and pummels them until the
    screams pour out freely,
while above them the roller coaster, before it plunges, creeps seemingly
    lost among its struts and braces
and under them the Ghost Train jerks through tunnels here and there
    lighted by fluorescent bones —
has fallen still today.

To us who live on Lavender Bay,
once Hulk Bay, before that no one now knows what,
it seemed the same easily frightened, big-lunged screamer cried out in
    mock terror each night across the water, and we hardly heard and
    took no notice.
But last night the screams pierced through dinner parties' laughter, and
    kept at it, until we sat up startled.

The Ghost Train, now carrying seven souls and the baffled grief of
    families,
has no special destination,
but must wander, looking for forgetfulness, through the natural world,
where all are born, all suffer, and many scream,
and no one is healed but gathered and used again.

THE GEESE

As soon as they come over the mountain
into the Connecticut Valley and see the river
they will follow until nightfall,
bodies, or cells, begin to tumble
between the streamers of their formation,
thinning the left, thickening the right,
until like a snowplowing skier the flock shifts weight
and shaking with its inner noises
turns, and yahonks and spirit-cries
toward that flow of light spelled into its windings
ages ago — each body flashing white
against the white sky when the wings lift,
and black when they fall, the invisible
continuously perforating the visible —
and trembles away, to vanish, but before that
to semi-vanish, as a mirage
or deepest desire does when it gets
the right distance from us and becomes rhythmic.

THE SHROUD

Lifted by its tuft
of angel hairs, a milkweed
seed dips-and-soars
across a meadow, chalking
in outline the rhythm
that waits in air all along,
like the bottom hem of nowhere.
Spinus tristis, who spends
his days turning gold
back into sod, rises-and-falls
along the same line the seed
just waved through the sunlight.
What sheet or shroud large enough
to hold the whole earth
are these seamstresses' chalks
and golden needles
stitching at so restlessly?
When will it ever be finished?

PART III

CHAMBERLAIN'S PORCH

On three sides of the stretcher bed
where I half sleep, rainwater runs down
boughs all broken out in buds out there
in the world the porch screen cuts up
into tiny, very perishable rectangles.
Rain putters down on the wood shingles overhead,
now smattering heavily, becoming a language,
now slackening, making kissing sounds
which some memorize even into the grave;
as though the mechanism governing the inner
pluckings of things, which goes forward forever,
pauses to try out its backward variations
on this wood-shingled porch roof in Connecticut.
Very distinctly, close to my ear,
a child's voice whispers "Grandpa!" A grandchild
still to be found? Or me, long ago,
calling an already lost grandfather?
Rain flurries down suddenly very thick,
overall batterings of the first shovelfuls
on a roof under which a body has stopped listening.

CEMETERY ANGELS

On these cold days
they stand over
our dead, who will
erupt into flower as soon
as memory and human shape
rot out of them, each bent
forward and with wings
partly opened as though
warming itself at a fire.

DECEMBER DAY IN HONOLULU

This day, twice as long as the same day in Sheffield, Vermont, where
    by five the stars come out,
gives the postman opportunity to boggle the bell thrice.
First, a letter from Providence lamenting the "siege against poets" —
    Wright, Rukeyser, Hayden.
Next, Richard Hugo's memoir of James Wright.
Last, around the time of stars in Sheffield, a package holding four glass
    doorknobs packed in a *New York Times* of a year ago, which
    Muriel Rukeyser had sea-mailed to me, to fulfill if not explain
    those mysterious words she used to whisper whenever we met:
    "Galway, I have your doorknobs."
The wail of a cat in heat — in ultraheat, here everything is hot
    already — breaks in, like the voice of propagation itself:
This one or that one dies but never the singer: whether in Honolulu in
    its humid mornings or in New York in its unbreathable dusk or in
    Sheffield now dark but for chimney sparks dying into the crowded
    heaven, one singer falls but the next steps into the empty place and
    sings . . .
The wail comes more heavily. Maybe propagation itself must haul its
    voice all the way up from the beginning.
Or it could be it's just a very old cat, clanking its last appearance on the
    magic circle of its trash can lid, from its final life crying back —
    before turning totally faithful forever — perhaps the first life's first
    irreplaceable lover.

ON THE OREGON COAST

In memoriam Richard Hugo

Six or seven rows of waves struggle landward.
The wind batters a pewtery sheen on the water between them.
As each wave makes its way in, most of it gets blown back out to sea,
    subverting even necessity.
The bass rumble of sea stones, audible when the waves flee all broken
    back out to sea, itself blows out to sea.
Now a log maybe thirty feet long and six across gets up and trundles
    down the beach.
Like a dog fetching a stick it flops unhesitatingly into the water.
An enormous wave at once sends it wallowing back up the beach again.
It lies among other driftwood, almost panting. Sure enough, after a few
    minutes it gets up, trundles down the beach, throws itself into the
    water again.
The last time I was on this coast Richard Hugo and I had dinner
    together just north of here, in a restaurant overlooking the sea.
The conversation came around to personification.
We agreed that eighteenth- and nineteenth-century poets almost *had* to
    personify, it was like mouth-to-mouth resuscitation, the only way
    they could imagine to keep the world from turning into dead
    matter.
And that as post-Darwinians it was up to us to anthropomorphize the
    world less and animalize, vegetable-ize, and mineralize ourselves
    more.
We doubted that pre-Darwinian language would let us.
Our talk turned to James Wright, how his kinship with salamanders,
    spiders, and mosquitoes allowed him to drift his way back through
    the evolutionary stages.
When a group of people gets up from a table, the table doesn't know
    which way any of them will go.

James Wright went back to the end. So did Richard Hugo.
The waves coming in burst up through their crests and fly very brilliant
back out to sea.
The log gets up yet again, goes rolling and bouncing down the beach,
plunges as though for good into the water.

LAST HOLY FRAGRANCE

In memoriam James Wright

When by first light I went out
from the last house on the chemin de Riou
to start up the cistern pump, there he sat,
mumbling into his notebook at an upstairs window
while the valley awakened: a cock
called full force, a car's gears
mis-shifted, a dog made some feeble yaps.
The next winter in Mt. Sinai, voiceless,
tufted with the stubble that sticks out
of chins on skid row in St. Paul,
Minnesota, he handed me the poem
of that Vence morning. Many times since,
I have said it and each time I have heard
his voice saying it under my voice,
and in fact in those auditoriums
that don't let you hear yourself, sometimes
I hear *only* his voice, edged, pitying,
surprising language with the mourning
that goes on inside it, for what it names,
making my eyes pop a little, perhaps
showing the whites, as his used to,
when his own poems startled him.
But poetry sings past even the sadness
that begins it: the drone of poetry readings
or the mutterings coming from poets' workrooms —
as oblivious to emotion as the printed page —
are only seeking that chant of the beginning,
older than any poem, that the song men
of Arnhem Land, who jolt their clapsticks
with a rebuking force like a spank, think

they summon, or the shaman in Point Barrow,
Alaska, having trance-learned it, translates,
or gopher frogs put to us in *parallelismus membrorum,*
or, now and then, a poem billows upon.
As do those last, saddest poems of his,
when they overtake the chant, synchronize
with its happiness, and, as when first light blooms
clouds of night, give us mourning's morning.
"How am I ever going to be able to say this?
The truth is there is something terrible,
almost unspeakably terrible in our lives,
and it demands respect, and, for some reason
that seems to me quite insane, it doesn't hate us.
There, you see? Every time I try
to write it down it comes out gibberish."
When the song goes, silence replaces it.
He lies back fast asleep in the airplane seat.
Under his eyelids consciousness flickers.
A computation: the difference, figured
in a flash, between what has been lived
and what remains to be. He dreams perhaps
of whittling a root, transfiguring it
by subtraction — of whatever it is in roots
that makes them cling — perhaps into a smile,
like that one now passing his lips, or into
a curled up, oriental death's body
mummified into the memories of last visitors.
Even asleep his face sweats. SS
torturers start working Cagney over. He knows
he will soon crack and spill the invasion plans.
Then he hears the rumbling of the B-24s
come to shut his mouth, and he cracks a grin.
When the bombs start exploding about him,
he throws back his head and madly laughs.
Sitting up, he peers out the plane window
to see if we might be coming in too low,
ready himself to laugh among the screams.
For this poet, the blessed moment

was not only at the end, in Fano, in spring,
where, with his beloved Annie, just before
returning home to die, he got well,
but also at first, forty years earlier,
by the Ohio, where he sat still and watched
the river flow, and flowed himself inside it,
humming and lulling first beginnings
that would heal not only his dumb-born self
but also the solitaries who sprawl on sidewalks
like dropped flowers waiting to be shoesoled
into first perfume or last stink, almost the same smell,
or squat in their own leakage on curbstones,
watching paper trash gyre and whirlwind
spellbound a block or so down East 12th Avenue
and fall back, trash again, or still stand
on a windy corner, gesticulating and talking
to nobody. The computation darkens.
Again and again it showed plenty of time.
Now, even on the abacus of the rosary,
or the petals, hushed to the tabletop, of roses,
which we mortal augurers figure and refigure
it out on our incredulous infinity of times,
it comes out: a negative number. Fear,
the potion of death, is yet a love derivative,
and some terrible pinch of it must be added
to restore the power to cling the penknife
gouges off the root. Near where it first forms,
the Ohio stops in its bed and baptizes under ice
all its creatures, even, in his anticipation,
the boy sitting soon in nobody's memory
some days downriver. He went away,
three-quarters whittled root of silenus wood,
taking a path that, had it simply vanished,
we could imagine keeps going, toward a place
where he waits in winding-cloth to rise again
into the religion of the idolatry of images
graven their moment into being-born-and-dying.
But the path ends there where a white rose

lies on top of its shadow in Martin's Ferry,
Ohio, let drop on her way to church by a child
too stunned by dead bells pounding through sunlight
to hold it, or anything, or anyone, tight
that day, giving up its last holy fragrance
into this ending-time, when the earth
lets itself be shoveled open to take in a body.
It will be a long time before anyone comes
who can lull the words he will not now ever use
— words which, now he has left, turn this way and that —
hum and coax them to press up against, shape
themselves by, know, true-love, and idolize.

THE PAST

A chair under one arm,
a desktop under the other,
the same Smith-Corona
on my back I even now batter
words into visibility with,
I would walk miles,
assemble my writing stall,
type all day, many sheets
of prose and verse all blown
away, while herring gulls
and once a sightseeing plane
turned overhead. The lean-
to of driftwood that thirty-
three-and-a-third years back
I put up on this spot
leans all the way down,
all its driftwood re-drifts.
Spray jumps and blows.
A few gulls fly that way,
a few this. A single duck
whettles out to sea
in straight flight — only vector
of purpose. As for the Quonset hut
I broke into without breaking it
when the storms came, it too
has gone, swept out, burned up,
buried under, nobody knows. Too
bad. But for me not all
that bad. For of the four
possibilities — from *me-and-it-*

still-here to *it-and-me-*
both-gone — this one, *me-here-*
it-gone, is second best,
and will do, for me, for now.
But I wanted it still to be here.
I wanted to sit at the table
and look up and see the sea spray
and beach grass happy together.
I wanted to remember the details:
the dingy, sprouted potatoes,
the Portuguese bread, the Bokar coffee,
the dyed oranges far from home,
the water tasting of decayed aluminum,
the kerosene stench. The front
steps where I sat and heard
the excitement that comes into sand,
the elation into poverty grass,
when the wind rises. In a letter
which cast itself down in General
Delivery, Provincetown, my friend
and mentor warned, "Don't lose
all touch with humankind." One day
while all around gulls whistled
their thin, exhausted screams,
the wind put down a sudden sheen
or flatness like spiritual quietness
across the water. Now two
waves of the North Atlantic
roll in side by side,
converge, ripple into one
and rush up the beach — making me
jump back — and vanish
under white bubbles all suddenly
popping away at once. Here
waves slap not in time
but in evanescence, a rhythmless medium.
Mere comings, mere goings. Though now
there's somewhat less coming

in the comings and considerably more
going in the goings. Between
the two straggles only
such an indicated boundary as the sea
lets the moon spell and die out
between world and world,
a wandering thread solitary walkers
follow along a beach, cross
and recross, spinning it
with their tracks all the way
into disappearance. So you see,
to reach the past is easy. A snap.
A snap of the sea and a third of a century
passes. All nothing. Or all all,
if that sounds more faithful. But anyway
all gone. The work of
whoziwhatzit — Zeit . . . Zman . . . Chas . . .
whatever . . . Whichever
you strike with the desperate tongue
gives a deadened sound, as though
the thing itself were fake; or unspeakable.

FIRST DAY OF THE FUTURE

They always seem to come up
on the future, these cold, earthly dawns;
the whiteness and the blackness
make the flesh shiver as though it's starting to break.
But that is always just an illusion,
always it is just another day they illuminate
of the permanent present. Except for today.
A motorboat sets out across the bay,
a transfiguring spirit, all its little puffy gasps
of disintegration collected
and anthemed out in a pure purr of dominion.
It disappears. In the stillness again
the shore lights remember the dimensions of the black water.
I don't know about this new life.
Even though I burned the ashes of its flag again and again
and set fire to the ticket that might have conscripted me into its ranks
and squandered my talents composing my emigration papers,
I think I want to go back now and live again in the present time, back
        there
where someone milks a cow and jets of intensest nourishment go squawk-
        ing into a pail,
where someone is hammering, a bit of steel at the end of a stick hitting
        a bit of steel, in the archaic stillness of an afternoon,
or somebody else saws a board, back and forth, like hard labor
in the lungs of one who refuses to come to the very end.
But I guess I'm here. So I must take care. For here
one has to keep facing the right way, or one sees one dies, and one dies.
I'm not sure I'm going to like it living here in the future.
I don't think I can keep on doing it indefinitely.

THE FUNDAMENTAL PROJECT
OF TECHNOLOGY

"A flash! A white flash sparkled!"
    Tatsuichiro Akizuki, Concentric Circles of Death

Under glass: glass dishes which changed
in color; pieces of transformed beer bottles;
a household iron; bundles of wire become solid
lumps of iron; a pair of pliers; a ring of skull-
bone fused to the inside of a helmet; a pair of eyeglasses
taken off the eyes of an eyewitness, without glass,
which vanished, when a white flash sparkled.

An old man, possibly a soldier back then,
now reduced down to one who soon will die,
sucks at the cigarette dangling from his lip, peers
at the uniform, scorched, of some tiniest schoolboy,
sighs out bluish mists of his own ashes over
a pressed tin lunch box well crushed back then when
the word *future* first learned, in a white flash, to jerk tears.

On the bridge outside, in navy black, a group
of schoolchildren line up, hold it, grin at a flash-pop,
scatter like pigeons across grass, see a stranger, cry
hello! hello! hello! and soon *goodbye! goodbye!*
having pecked up the greetings that fell half unspoken
and the going-sayings that those who went the day
it happened a white flash sparkled did not get to say.

If all a city's faces were to shrink back all at once
from their skulls, would a new sound come into existence,
audible above moans eaves extract from wind that smoothes
the grass on graves, or raspings heart's-blood greases still,
or wails infants trill born already skillful at the grandpa's rattle,

or infra-screams bitter-knowledge's speechlessness
memorized, at that white flash, inside closed-forever mouths?

To de-animalize human mentality, to purge it of obsolete
evolutionary characteristics, in particular of death,
which foreknowledge terrorizes the contents of skulls with,
is the fundamental project of technology; however,
pseudologica fantastica's mechanisms require:
to establish deathlessness it is necessary to eliminate
those who die; a task attempted, when a white flash sparkled.

Unlike the trees of home, which continually evaporate
along the skyline, the trees here have been enticed down
toward world-eternity. No one knows which gods they enshrine.
Does it matter? Awareness of ignorance is as devout
as knowledge of knowledge. Or more so. Even though not knowing,
sometimes we weep, from surplus of gratitude, even though knowing,
twice already on earth sparkled a flash, a white flash.

The children go away. By nature they do. And by memory,
in scorched uniforms, holding tiny crushed lunch tins.
All the ecstasy-groans of each night call them back, satori
their ghostliness back into the ashes, in the momentary shrines,
the thankfulness of arms, from which they will go
again and again, until the day flashes and no one lives
to look back and say, a flash, a white flash sparkled.

THE WAKING

What has just happened between the lovers,
who lie now in love-sleep under the memory
of owls calling in the deeper love-sleep of the woods —
call exhaled, *answer* inhaled, *call* exhaled,
answer inhaled, back and forth, and so on,
until one, calling faster, overtakes the other
and the two suddenly whoo together in a single
shimmering harmonic — is called "lovemaking."
But lovers who come exalted to their trysts,
who come to each other from opposite directions
along a path by the sea, through the pines,
meet, embrace, go up from the sea,
make love, lie crushed into each other
under the all-golden sky already deep-blueing
its moon and stars into shining, know
they don't "make" love, which is, was, will be,
but are earth-creatures chosen by moon-pull
to live and flow and — here no other word will do —
fuck one another forever if possible across the stars.
But this word, perhaps first heard when lovers
dropped a stone into the sea at night
and out in the dark a mullet leapt and fell back,
sounding an answer that reverberated in them,
has had the map of the almost-last pathway left
craving its way back to the beginning scuffed out of it.
The true word, if it exists, exists inside the tongue
and from there must make language, consciousness,
even all of forgetting, remember: as when
flamingoes change feeding places on a marsh
and there is a moment — after the first to fly

has put its head underwater in the new place
and before in the old place the last
lifts its head sees the rest have gone —
when, scattered with pink bodies, the sky
becomes all one vast remembering. They still hear,
in the distance, the steady crushing and uncrushing
of bedsprings; and perhaps only imagine a sonata
in which violins' lines remember into the room
the writhing and shifting of sexual bodies.
The already-memory of what has just happened
is their *déjà-prévu* of the existence
of existence. They lie with heads touching,
thinking themselves back across the blackness
that converts back to use of world-light
those who have lived one moment by love-light.
On the brightening sheet their bodies re-form
— golden heaps the true embrace sluices
out of the night. The bed, caressed threadbare,
worn almost away, is now one more place
where such inner light as humans can hold
glimmers into us. The eyelids,
which love the eyes and must lie on them to sleep,
open: *This is a bed. That is a fireplace.*
That is last morning's breakfast tray,
which nobody has yet bothered to take away.
This face — too rich in feeling to have lived past
the world in which it is said, "Ni vous sans moi,
ni moi sans vous," so blatantly archaic
this day might be breaking in the Middle Ages —
is the illusion randomness finally chooses
to smile into existence, now, on this pillow.
The lovers don't have words to know this through.
The scraps of poetry they do have mean less
in the in-the-tongue language than "want a cracker"
or "pieces of eight" in ours. Through tears
they see more truly than the dry-eyed the motes
cross, mingle, collide, lose their way, in this puff
of ecstatic dust. Now the tears overwhelm the eyes,

wet their faces, drain quickly away
into their smiles. One leg hangs off the bed.
He is still inside her. His big toe
sticks into the pot of strawberry jam. "Oh migod!"
They laugh. They have to remind themselves how to.
They kiss while laughing and hit teeth
and remember they are bones and at once laugh
naturally again. A clock is ticking. The feeling —
perhaps it is only a feeling, perhaps due
to living always in the same lifetime
with only dying things — that time passes,
comes over them. They get up,
put on clothes, go out. They are not in the street
yet, however, but for a few moments longer
still in their elsewhere, on a riverbank
standing with their arms around each other in the aura
the earth has when it remembers its former beauty.
Something in them — the past — belongs
to the away-going water and must spill
into time to come forever. It does not yet surprise them
that they are wood-nymph and river-spirit,
who can speak for mute things and name them.
River birds . . . honk. Sounds arrive fully formed
into their mouths . . . *Bleecker* . . . *Carmine* . . . *Avenue
of the Americas* . . . An ambulance sirens
a shroud-whitened body toward St. Vincent's.
A police car running the red lights parodies
in high pitch the owls of paradise. The lovers enter
the ordinary day the ordinary world
providentially provides. Their pockets ring.
Good. For now askers and beggarmen
come up to them needing change for breakfast.

THAT SILENT EVENING

I will go back to that silent evening
when we lay together and talked in low, silent voices,
while outside slow lumps of soft snow
fell, hushing as they got near the ground,
with a fire in the room, in which centuries
of tree went up in continuous ghost-giving-up,
without a crackle, into morning light.
Not until what hastens went slower did we sleep.
When we came back we turned and looked back
at our tracks, where they lie still across the land
of our twining, twining out of the woods
where the branches we brushed against let fall
puffs of sparkling snow, quickly, in silence,
like stolen kisses, and where the *scritch scritch scritch*
among the trees, which is the sound that dies
inside the sparks that shoot from the wedge when the sledge
hits it off center telling everything inside
it is fire, jumped to a black branch, all puffed up
and without arms, and so obviously lonesome,
and yet — how could we know this? — *happy!*
in shape of chickadee. Lying still in snow,
not iron-willed, like railroad tracks, willing
not to meet until heaven, but here and there
making stomped, slubby kissing-knots in the snow,
our tracks wobble across the field their long scratch.
Everything that happens here — even in the cold air
the chick when at last grown old *dee dee dees*
through — is really little more, if even that,
than a scratch, too. Words, in our mouths,
are almost ready, already, to bandage the one

whom the *scritch scritch scritch*, meaning *if how when*
we will lose each other, scratches scratches scratches
from this moment to that. Then I will go back
to that silent evening, when the past just managed
to cross into the future, if just by a trace, and the light
that lives inside the overlap doubles and shines
through the dark the sparkling that heavens the earth.

THE SEEKONK WOODS

When first I walked here I hobbled
along ties set too close together
for a boy to step naturally on each.
When I grew older, I thought, my stride
would reach every other and thereafter
I would walk in time with the way
toward the meeting place of rails
in that yellow Lobachevskian haze up ahead.
Right about here we put down our pennies, dark
on shined steel, where they trembled, fell still,
and waited for the locomotive rattling berserk
wheel-rods into perfect circles out of Attleboro
to brighten them into wafers, the way a fork
mashes into view the inner light of a carrot
in a stew. In this late March sunshine,
crossing the trees at the angle the bow makes
when it effleurages out of the chanterelle
the C three octaves above middle C,
the old vertical birthwood remembers
its ascent lines, shrunken by half, exactly
back down, each tree's on its fallen last summer.
Back then, these rocks often asked
blood offerings — but this one, once, bone, too,
the time Billy Wallace tripped and broke out
his front teeth. Fitted with gold replicas,
he asked, speaking more brightly, "What good
is a golden mouth when there's only grass
to eat?" Though it was true Nebuchadnezzar
spent seven years down on all fours
eating vetch and alfalfa, ruminating

the mouth-feel of "bloom" and "wither,"
until he was healed, nevertheless we knew
if you held a grass blade between both thumbs
and blew hard you could blurt all its shrieks
out of it — like those beseechings leaves oaks
didn't drop last winter just now scratched out
on a breeze, let-me-die-let-me-die.
Maybe Billy, lured by bones' memory,
comes back sometimes, too, to the Seekonk Woods,
to stand in the past and just look at it.
Here he might kneel, studying this clump of grass,
as a god might inspect a human sneeze
that percusses through. Or he might stray
into the now untrafficked whistling-lanes
of the mourning doves, who used to call and call
into the future, and give a start, as though,
this very minute, by awful coincidence,
they reach it. And at last traipse off
down the tracks, with arrhythmic gait,
as wanderers must do once it hits them:
the over-the-unknown route, too, ends up
where time wants. On this spot
I skinned the muskrat. I buried the rat.
The musk breezed away. Of the fur
I made a hat, which as soon as put on
began to rot off, and even now stinks
so sharply my scalp crawls. In circles,
of course, keeping to the skull. Though
one day this scrap of damp skin
will crawl all the way off, and the whole organism
follow. But which way? To effuse with musk?
Or rot with rat? When, a quarter-
turn after the sun, the half-moon,
too, goes down and we find ourselves
in the night's night, then somewhere
thereabouts in the dark must be death.
Knowledge beforehand of it is surely among
existence's most spectacular feats — and yet right here,

on this ordinary afternoon, in these woods,
with a name meaning "black goose" in Wampanoag,
or in modern Seekonkese, "slob blowing fat nose,"
this unlikely event happens — a creature
walking the tracks knows it will come.
Then too long to touch every tie, my stride
is now just too short to reach every other,
and so I am to be still the wanderer, the hobble
of too much replaced by the common limp
of too little. But I almost got there.
I almost stepped according to the liturgical,
sleeping gods' snores you can hear singing up
from former times inside the ties. I almost
set foot in that border zone where what follows
blows back, shimmering everything, making
walking like sleepwalking, railroad tracks
a lane among poplars on a spring morning,
where a man, limping but blissful, dazedly
makes his way homeward, his lips, which kissing
taught to bunch up like that, blowing
from a night so overfilled with affection
it still hasn't completely finished passing
these few bent strands of hollowed-out air,
haunted by future, into a tune on the tracks.
I think I'm about to be shocked awake.
As I was in childhood, when I battered myself
back to my senses against a closed door,
or woke up hanging out of an upstairs window.
Somnambulism was my attempt to slip
under cover of nightmare across no father's land
and put my arms around a phantasm. If only
I had found a way to enter his hard time
served at labor by day, by night in solitary,
and put my arms around him in reality,
I might not now be remaking him
in memory still; anti-alchemizing bass kettle's
golden reverberations again and again back down
to hair, flesh, blood, bone, the base metals.

I want to crawl face down in the fields
and graze on the wild strawberries, my clothes
stained pink, even for seven years
if I must, if they exist. I want to lie out
on my back under the thousand stars and think
my way up among them, through them,
and a little distance past them, and attain
a moment of nearly absolute ignorance,
if I can, if human mentality lets us.
I have always intended to live forever,
but even more, to live now. The moment
I have done one or the other, I here swear,
I will come back from the living and enter
death everlasting: consciousness abandoned.
And I will not offer to burn my words.
The poplar logs creosoted asleep under the tracks
have stopped snoring. Maybe they're waking up.
The bow saws at G. A leaf rattles on its branch.
The rails may never meet, O fellow Euclideans,
for you, for me. Never mind if we groan.
That is our noise. Laughter is our stuttering
in a language we can't speak yet. Behind,
the world made of wishes goes dark. Ahead,
if not now then never, shines only what is.

ACKNOWLEDGMENTS

INDEX

ACKNOWLEDGEMENTS

Many of the poems in this volume were originally published in the following magazines, journals, and books:

BODY RAGS

Choice: "Mango" and "Testament of the Thief"; *Colorado State Review:* "Getting the Mail"; *The Hudson Review:* "The Porcupine"; *The Minor Bird:* "The Falls"; *The Nation:* "Last Songs" and "Night in the Forest"; *The New Yorker:* "The Fossils" and "La Bagarède"; *The Paris Review:* "Another Night in the Ruins"; *Poetry:* "The Last River" (under the title "The Mystic River"), "The Correspondence School Instructor Says Goodbye to His Poetry Students," "The Poem," "In the Anse Galet Valley," "How Many Nights," and "In the Farmhouse"; *A Poetry Reading Against the Vietnam War:* "Vapor Trail Reflected in the Frog Pond"; *The Sixties:* "Going Home by Last Light" and "The Bear."

MORTAL ACTS, MORTAL WORDS

The American Poetry Review: "Angling, a Day," "On the Tennis Court at Night," "The Last Hiding Places of Snow," and "The Sadness of Brothers"; *Chicago Review:* "The Still Time"; *Choice:* "After Making Love We Hear Footsteps"; *Country Journal:* "Kissing the Toad"; *Field:* "Looking at Your Face"; *Harper's:* "There Are Things I Tell to No One"; *Harvard Magazine:* "Blackberry Eating"; *Iowa Review:* "Fisherman"; *Kenyon Review:* "Goodbye" and "Lava"; *Mississippi Review:* "52 Oswald Street"; *Missouri Review:* "The Apple"; *New England Review:* "In the Bamboo Hut"; *New Letters:* "Brother of My Heart"; *The New Republic:* "Les Invalides"; *The New Yorker:* "Daybreak," "Fergus Falling," "The Apple Tree," "The Choir," "The Gray Heron," "Saint Francis and the Sow," and "Wait"; *The New York Review of Books:* "Flying Home"; *The Paris Review:* "The Milk Bottle"; *The Three Rivers Poetry Journal:* "Memory of Wilmington."

The American Poetry Review: "The Fundamental Project of Technology," "On the Oregon Coast," and "The Waking"; *Antaeus:* "Conception," "December Day in Honolulu," "Driftwood from a Ship," and "The Man Splitting Wood in the Daybreak"; *Apparitions:* "Cemetery Angels" and "Farm Picture"; *The Atlantic:* "The Past"; *Kenyon Review:* "Fire in Luna Park" and "Last Holy Fragrance"; *Mother Jones:* "The Road Between Here and There"; *The Nation:* "Break of Day" and "Prayer"; *New Letters:* "The Olive Wood Fire"; *The New Yorker:* "First Day of the Future," "Middle of the Night," "The Seekonk Woods," and "The Shroud"; *The Paris Review:* "Chamberlain's Porch," "The Frog Pond," "The Geese," and "The Old Life"; *Scripsi:* "The Ferry Stopping at MacMahon's Point"; *Southwest Review:* "Milk"; *Verse:* "The Angel" and "The Sow Piglet's Escapes."

INDEX

Galway Kinnell lives part of the time in New York City, where he is Erich Maria Remarque Professor of Creative Writing at New York University, and part of the time in Vermont. Beside his books of poetry he has published a novel, *Black Light*, a book of interviews, *Walking down the Stairs*, a children's book, *How the Alligator Missed Breakfast*, and translations of the poetry of François Villon, Yvan Goll, and Yves Bonnefoy, and edited *The Essential Whitman*. He has been a MacArthur Fellow. His *Selected Poems* won the Pulitzer Prize and, with Charles Wright's *Country Music*, the American Book Award.